Hillside Golf Club

— Out Of The Shadows —

1911 - 2011

Harry Foster

Hillside Golf Club
Out Of The Shadows
1911 - 2011

By
Harry Foster

Hillside Golf Club 2011

Hillside Golf Club 2011

First Published in the United Kingdom in 2011
By Hillside Golf Club
Southport.

© The Hillside Golf Club

All rights reserved.
No part of this publication may be
reproduced, stored in any retrieval system,
or transmitted in any form or by any means
electronic, mechanical, photocopying, recording
or otherwise, without the prior permission
of the copyright owner.

ISBN No. 978-0-9567586-0-6

Typeset in Century Gothic 10pt

Cover photograph courtesy of
www.kevinmurraygolfphotography.com © 2010

Printed and Published for Hillside Golf Club
by Custom Print Limited
13-23 Naylor Street, Liverpool, England.

Hillside Golf Club

― Out Of The Shadows ―

1911 - 2011

Published in a limited edition of 1000 copies

310/1000

Harry Foster

Custom Print Limited, England 2011

Author's Acknowledgments

Hillside Golf Club does not have an organised archive of photographs and memorabilia, although a limited amount of material does exist. The most important surviving item is a brief history in a scrapbook, which appears to have been assembled in 1976. In addition to the text it contains membership cards, photographs and maps. The cards had been issued to Bert Collinge, who joined the Club in 1919 and was to become one of its most influential members, which suggests that he might have been involved in this compilation. The collection of surviving committee minutes is incomplete and there are none for the period prior to 1923.

In the 1980s Philip Irlam undertook to write a history of the Club's first eighty years – *A Lively Octogenarian, Hillside Golf Club 1911-1991*. His researches revealed the extent (and the limitations) of the existing material. I have worked my way through this material and I am grateful to him for the sign posts that his diligent labours provided. As an active local historian I have also been able to consult the archives of other local golf clubs and bodies, along with landowners' and local authority records that inform much of the Club's history. I have attempted to sound out members and others for their memories and I am grateful to all who have taken the trouble to assist in this process and to make illustrations available. They have included: Rita Abberley, Derek Anderson, John Ball, Stuart Brown, Gerry Brunskill, Barry Coyne, the late Tony Crane, Tony Coop, Nigel Dixon, Sheelah Foulds, John Graham, Graham and Pam Green, Bryan Greenwood, Robert Godley, Jan Hewitt, Keith Hick, Derek Holden, Gordon Hughes, Harold James, the late Tom Johnson, Bernie, Brian and Phillip Kenyon, Chris Leather, Tom Murray, John Nelson, Jean Priestley, Mark Prue, Pam Roberts, Tom Rooney, John Scriarrni, Brian Seddon, John Simmons, Pat Smillie, Brian Street, Gary Taylor, George Tomlinson, Ann Turnbull, Martin Twist, Mike Wall, Alan Whittaker and Paul Wisse (Senior Officer, Sefton Coastal Defence). There will be other contributions which I have inadvertently failed to acknowledge, for which I apologise. Importantly, Alan Birch and Martin Lockeyer have produced photographs of current activity at the Club. Images have also been provided by The Southport Reference Library, the Sefton Coastal Defence Project and the Birkdale and Ainsdale Historical Research Society. The Ordnance Survey mapping included within this publication is provided by the Sefton Council under licence from the Ordnance Survey in order to fulfil its public function to support local history and culture.

Completing this book has been facilitated by the co-operation and contributions of the Club's secretary/manager Simon Newland and his assistants. Coffee pleasantly delivered to 'my study' in the Board Room, by the catering staff, has been much appreciated. Gerry Brunskill and Graham Green have been towers of strength in this endeavour and the diligence of Pauline Horner has ensured proper account being taken of Hillside ladies. As ever my most profound thanks go to my wife Thelma, who has had to live through, and proof read, the twelve books that I have written since I retired.

I have enjoyed a long and happy relationship with the Hillside Club. I played on the pre-1967 course and had the good fortune to share a win during that era in the men's invitation whilst playing with the late George Bromilow. Little did I think then, that some 50 years later I would enjoy the privilege and pleasure of writing a history of this great Club.

Hillside Golf Club
Out Of The Shadows
1911 - 2011

Author's Acknowledgements		
Foreword	Peter Alliss	
Preface	The Captain –	
	The Lady Captain –	
Chapter One	Introduction	1
Chapter Two	The Beginnings: Hill Side Farm 1911-1923	5
Chapter Three	The Guardians and the Anxious Years 1923-1967	15
Chapter Four	A New Course and Clubhouse 1923-1967	23
Chapter Five	Professional Tournaments 1923-1967 With a contribution by Jack Nicklaus	40
Chapter Six	Club Matters at Hillside 1923-1967	50
Chapter Seven	A Championship Course 1967-2010	70
Chapter Eight	A Tournament Venue of Choice 1967-2010	83
Chapter Nine	Club Professionals, Champions and Championships 1967-2010	99
Chapter Ten	Social Hillside 1967-2010	121
Chapter Eleven	Hillside Centenary 2011	129
Bibliography		139
Honours Board		140

The Author

Harry Foster

Harry Foster has lived in Southport all his life. He attended KGV School, where a number of Hillside members, including Michael Buckles, were his peers. His first teaching post was at Farnborough Road Junior School and many who were, or were to become, members of Hillside were among his pupils, they included Steve Rooke and Michael Pearson, who were exhibiting a passion for golf at an early age. Later, as head of department at Edge Hill College he was involved in teacher education and some half a dozen of his colleagues, at the College, were Hillside members. Since the 1960s Harry has enjoyed strong links with the Hillside Club, playing the course regularly, on one occasion losing to Gordon Rimmer and John Ball in the third or fourth round of the Daily Mail Foursomes Competition.

For over forty years Harry has lectured and given talks on many aspects of local history and has obtained a master's degree and a Ph.D. from the University of Liverpool for local research. Since retiring he has had twelve books on various aspects of local history published, including one on Birkdale and one on Ainsdale.

Harry has been a member of the Hesketh Golf Club since the 1960s and was the captain in 1995. Having written a critically acclaimed regional study of the development of golf - Links Along the Line – he was in a strong position to write The Annals of Hesketh Golf Club in 2000 and Southport and Ainsdale: The Golfer' Club 1906-2006 for their centenary year. In the most unusual circumstances, which Gerry Brunskill might be persuaded to reveal, he accepted an invitation to write a centenary history of Hillside. Harry has also spent some two years studying the archives of the Royal Birkdale Golf Club.

A family man, Harry shares his hobbies of walking, bird watching and golf with his wife, although the passing years have diminished the energy levels for these activities. He is a member and past president of the Southport Rotary Club. An enthusiastic sportsman, Harry was a member of a successful championship winning Lancashire County rugby team in the 1950s and was a reserve for the England XV, in those distant days before squads, substitutes, international under 21 and A teams, and national team tours. Hillside's illustrious rugby international, Gordon Rimmer, his club captain at Waterloo and colleague in the Lancashire team, acted as chauffeur and mentor to a very raw young nineteen year old, when he made the transition from the playing field at KGV to Twickenham.

Foreword

Peter Alliss
10 June 2009

If England has a golfing coastline to compare with the Costa del Sol, it's that wondrous stretch from the Wirral in Cheshire to Blackpool in Lancashire – magnificent links interspersed with delightful inland golf courses, which have been the source of great pleasure for generations. It's an area very well known to the Alliss family; my father played in many tournaments and the Ryder Cup in the early 1930s, and I followed in his footsteps competing in numerous events and Ryder Cups, some of which brought pleasure, others an occasional tear!

There would be truth in saying that Hillside was, for many years, a sleeping giant. Located as it is between Southport and Ainsdale and Royal Birkdale, it lived for years in their considerable 'shadows', but gradually the reputation of the course grew, to such a degree that it has now staged many of Britain's top golfing events both professional and amateur, men and women.

Years ago deposits of the finest quality sand, required for the manufacture of glass, were discovered beneath the course, much excavation was carried out and for a number of years there was disruption. But the course has gradually settled and now stands alongside the best of Britain's links courses. I can't think of a more formidable set of opening holes than those at Hillside, particularly with nerves a little raw and a strong wind blowing from right to left, urging the slightest wayward tee shots on to the railway line, which is exceedingly greedy and gobbles balls at an alarming rate!

Hilda and Fred Wormald, dear friends, lived less than a hundred yards from the club house, and every time professional golf was played in the area their house became my 'home from home'. I visited the club many times. John Burton was the professional. His brother, Richard, had won the Open Championship at St Andrews in 1939 and due to the war years held the title longer than anyone else in the history of the game! Many thought John a dour character, tall and craggy, but beneath the sombre exterior was a good sense of humour. He was most concerned members shouldn't think that he was doing too well financially, and most days he arrived on his 'sit up and beg' bicycle. When he bought a new car it was months before it was put on public show. It was even rumoured that on the rare occasions that he took his wife out socially he adopted a disguise just in case one of the members should spot him out and report back to the club!

Hillside Golf Club has many of the wonderful qualities that make British golf clubs so special, and, I'm sure, that's the way it will continue for years to come.

Congratulations on your Centenary.

Preface

The Captain – Alan Harkness

I am privileged to have been asked to contribute to this publication marking the fantastic milestone of the club's centenary year in 2011. It is a book I hope will be of interest not only to our members but also to golf enthusiasts further afield.

I must acknowledge the vast amount of work that has gone into producing this book and thank the prime movers who have been working on it for several years, Graham Green and his Centenary Committee and, of course, the author, Dr Harry Foster.

Hillside remains one of the top clubs in the country with an outstanding course and clubhouse. This is no fluke - it is a result of the hard work and dedication shown by all committee members, board members and green staffs, not just currently but throughout the last 100 years. Guests and visitors are always welcomed and consistently praise Hillside's facilities; indeed, as a member myself for the past 20 years, all my guests have commented that this is one of their all-time favourite courses.

The club also works hard to promote a thriving junior section. This is an important investment as it will ensure that the club is in good hands heading towards its bi-centennial.

I look forward to all the events and centenary celebrations planned for this coming year, from the formal gatherings to Hillside's own traditional hickory golf club competition.

I hope you enjoy reading this fascinating history of the club and I look forward to welcoming members, guests and visitor to Hillside Golf Club in our Centennial Year.

Finally, I would like to dedicate this book to all the unpaid committee members who have guided the club over the last century.

The Lady Captain – Jane E S Rose

I am delighted to have been elected Lady Captain for this the Centenary Year 2011.

Not only do I consider it a great honour to have been chosen for this role by the present Lady Captains, I feel highly privileged to be a member of such a well respected club and to uphold the many fine traditions and standards which we have inherited.

Our ladies' section has grown from strength to strength not only in membership but in our playing ability and we are now proudly fielding five teams each season, from Scratch, through to Shield/Handicap, Bronze, Third and Millennium, not forgetting our well established and thriving bridge team. Of course this would not be possible without the unstinting time and work undertaken by the officers and committee members - from those whose foresight and tenacity have enabled a ladies' membership to exist at all, to those who still tirelessly work for the Hillside Golf Club ladies' section now.

It is with great excitement and anticipation that I look forward to playing a part in our Club's history and to participate in the many proposed events during this special year.

I know that you will enjoy reading this book and hope that you will spend many happy years playing golf here at Hillside.

Jane Rose

Fig.1 *Sun Alliance PGA Pro Am 1982.*
Hillside Captain John McAlister (second left) playing with Greg Norman (right).

Chapter One
Introduction

Hillside is currently regarded as probably Great Britain's finest links golf course not to have hosted the Open Championship. Australian Wayne Riley, a TV commentator and formerly a successful tournament player expressed this view after playing the course in 2001. Writing in 1991, Peter Alliss described Hillside as '…one of the most scenic and testing links courses in the British Isles' and concluded that: 'There is NO doubt the Hillside course could host the Open Championship.' Double Open Champion Australian Greg Norman, graciously wrote an unsolicited note to the Club after playing in the PGA tournament at Hillside in 1982 (Fig.1) stating that: 'The back nine holes are the best in Britain.' He was later to say that in his view the Hillside course was '…second only to Augusta'. Jack Nicklaus described the course as '…a wild looking links' and added that '…within the second half are some of my favourite holes.' He had made his professional debut in Britain at Hillside in 1962 and has generously supplied a substantial contribution for this centenary book (see chapter 5). Current confirmation of these assessments from leading golfers comes from national and international golf magazines, which annually rank the top courses. Hillside consistently figures strongly in such lists. The Royal and Ancient Golf Club of St Andrews added its endorsement by awarding Hillside the prestigious Amateur Championship for a second time in 2011, the Club's centenary year.

The Club has also developed a clubhouse worthy of its status, whilst on the course the members, ladies, men, and juniors, have established a strong regional reputation for golfing excellence.

The story so far might hardly seem to fit a club, which the title of this book describes as having emerged from 'Out of the Shadows' but in succeeding chapters I will try to demonstrate its aptness. After deciding upon this title, I was encouraged to discover that in 1969 an eminent golf journalist, Tom Scott, had written that Hillside had been out of golf's limelight but was now '…more than ready to take its place in the sun.' Peter Alliss, whose association with the Club goes back many years, expresses a similar view in his 2009 contribution to this centenary book.

The first shadow is, however, that of doubt. Seldom can the precise beginnings of a major club have been as shrouded in mystery as appears to be the case with Hillside Golf Club. Sadly there are no Club records available for the years prior to 1923 to clarify the issue. Reports in local newspapers frequently compensate for an absence of archives, but not in the case of Hillside. It was, perhaps, this void and the apparently low-key nature of the Club's early years that prompted R. Endersby Howard, writing in a Hillside Club handbook published in 1932, to suggest that the Club '…has little history.'

A surviving membership ticket confirms that the 'Hillside Golf Club' was in existence in April 1913 (Fig.2). But how was 1911 identified as the foundation year? *The Golfers' Handbook*, which began to record club foundation dates in 1959, incorrectly listed Hillside as having been formed in 1925 and in 1962 the date was amended to 1911. A later enquiry to the publisher of this handbook revealed that this change was made at the behest of the Club, which would have had the opportunity to revise the previous year's entry before the annual publication. Early members of the Club could still have been consulted in 1962. One such member, who contributed when a scrapbook history of the Club was assembled in 1976 was H.S. (Bert) Collinge, who had joined the Club in 1919, was captain for the second time in 1962 and was chairman between 1953 and 1967, and as such he would have been involved in making the 1962 alteration of the date in *The Golfers' Handbook* from '1925' to '1911'. At the Annual General Meeting (AGM) in 1961 he announced that: '1962 would be the Club's 50th jubilee year.' Earlier The Society of Liverpool Golf Captains, when promulgating a new constitution in 1939, incorrectly included the Club's date of origin as 1923, the year that Hillside Golf Club Limited was incorporated. This entry was also later amended to 1911.

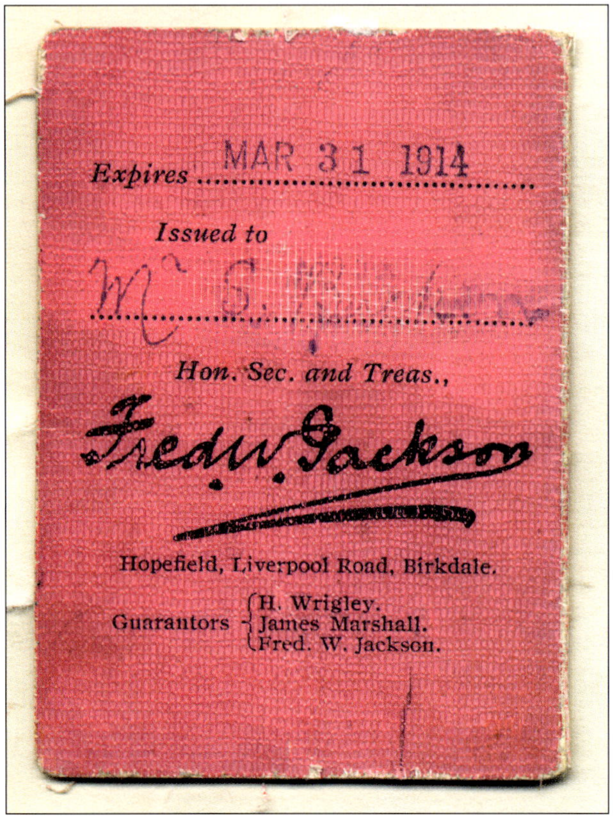

Fig.2 *Hillside Golf Club membership ticket 1913. This earliest known Hillside artefact is pasted into a brief scrapbook history of the Club.*

What other evidence might help to confirm 1911 as the date? Hillside is one of an extraordinary cluster of internationally famous championship golf links on the south-west Lancashire coast. Henry Longhurst described this area as '…a sandy paradise that stretches for miles along the coast between Liverpool and Southport.' For Bernard Darwin it was '…a noble stretch of golfing ground that is second to none.' It was the building of a railway line from Liverpool to Southport in the middle of the 19th century, which was to transform this previously sparsely populated coastal strip. The middle classes were quitting their suburbs on the immediate fringes of the city, fleeing both the smoke and the remorseless advance of Liverpool's people-teeming terraces. The availability of regular and rapid transport meant that the land along this northern line became an attractive proposition for commuters. Nature, in the form of a south-westerly prevailing wind, contributed fresh clean air and the landowners ensured that their new high-class residential estates offered the social seclusion so valued by the middle classes.

The railway line runs along the inland margin of what is arguably the finest tract of coastal sand-dunes in the country. This strip is over ten miles long and in places over a mile in depth. The first golf club to be formed along the line was the West Lancashire Golf Club at Blundellsands in 1869. Formby Golf Club was founded in 1884 and played on 'The Warren' at Freshfield. A month later the Southport (Hesketh) Golf Club followed on the Marshside Hills, the northern end of the dune coast, where sandhills give way to Ribble marshes. This club was brought into being by members of the local social elite, who lived mainly in the Hesketh Park and Birkdale Park areas, Southport's high-class residential suburbs. It was largely Birkdale Park residents amongst the Southport members who four years later formed the Birkdale Club, with a nine-hole course on Shaw's Hills, part of which is now Bedford Park. Birkdale moved to its present links in 1897, and Hesketh (Southport), after a brief stay at a course which was later occupied by the YMCA then the Old Links golf clubs, returned to the Marshside Hills links in 1902, Thus in the early years of the 20th century there were two well-established golf clubs in the Southport area, but membership was expensive and there was a demand for access to golf from a wider public. The responses to this demand shed further light on the origins of Hillside Golf Club.

Fig.3 Hill Side Farm course 1907. The first tenant club, 'The Grosvenor', was briefly known as 'Southport Golf Club' and then became 'Southport and Ainsdale'. This section of an OS map extends to include the former 'Birkdale Golfing Course' on Shaw's Hills, part of which survives as Bedford Park.

It was in January 1906 that 42 members of a whist club, based on the Smedley Hydro in Grosvenor Road, Birkdale, met to consider forming a golf club. Within a month the Grosvenor Golf Club was founded and had rented part of Peter Lloyd's Hill Side Farm for a course (Fig.3). The site of Hill Side Farm is now a cul-de-sac between numbers 33 to 45 Dunbar Road. The course was on a 30-acre triangle of land immediately inland of the railway line that stretched south from the original but long-closed Birkdale railway station, beyond Conyers Avenue, to what was to become Hillside Station. A modest wooden pavilion was erected alongside the railway, close to the old station and access was from the present Birkdale station along Dover Road, or by the path from the tram terminus at the Smedley Hydro, which crossed the railway line at Gilbert's Crossing. By October the number of members had grown to 140 making the small course congested and the Club agreed to lease approximately 100 acres from Weld-Blundell for an 18-hole course. This course, to the south and east of Hill Side Farm, was opened for play in May 1907. During the Club's first year its name was changed three times. These names briefly included 'Southport Golf Club', as shown on the Ordnance Survey map, before it finally became the Southport and Ainsdale Golf Club (S&A).

The abandoned nine-hole course was not allowed to lie fallow for long. In July 1907 W.A. Findlay, a Scottish dentist with a Southport town-centre practice, rented the course in his own name. A local politician, he wanted to provide golf without '…burdening the members with the heavy expenses usually associated with the game.' He had already founded the Southport Athletic Golf Club near the tram terminus at Blowick, which charged members a fee of five shillings (25p) a year. His new club, at Hill Side Farm was known as the Blundell Golf Club and the annual fee was set at a guinea (£1.05) only half of the S&A figure; the joining fee was a fifth of that at S&A and a tenth of those of the Birkdale and Hesketh clubs. Like S&A, the Blundell campaigned actively to attract members. Local newspapers, which gave good coverage to golf, contained promotional articles and the clubs also inserted adverts.

Advice from Peter McEwan, the professional at Hesketh Golf Club, led to some course alterations at Hill Side. The Blundell Club prospered and by October 1907 the membership had reached 185 men and 105 ladies. A number of these members lived in the Liverpool area, and were able to get a special rate on the railway; the *Southport Visiter* reported that: 'Many Liverpool golfers wanting cheap golf have found out the merits of the Blundell Club.' Regular team matches were played between teams drawn from the Club's Liverpool and Southport residents. By 1911, it appears that the Blundell Club had also outgrown this course and on the 7th March 1911 it played its last medal there and moved to a new nine-hole course, on land to the south of Ainsdale Station, which was leased from landowner Charles Weld-Blundell. The new course, which was approached from Chesterfield Road, was opened on the 5th April.

The small Hill Side Farm course was once again abandoned. W.A. Findlay, who was a Southport town councillor, was also the champion of the campaign to establish a municipal golf course in the town. Eventually, in 1911, his persistence appears to have persuaded his fellow councillors of the merits of his case. In seeking a site for a municipal course the newly vacant Hill Side Farm course was seriously considered but after a meeting in February 1911, between the Corporation's representatives and landowner's agent, it was rejected in favour of reclaimed foreshore at the northern end of the Promenade, where space was not a problem and a nine-hole course, which would be later enlarged to 18 holes, was opened in 1912.

The residents of Dunkirk Road were afraid that the former course on Hill Side Farm would be built upon and in September 1911 they petitioned the Town Council that it should be retained as open land. In his 1991 account of the first 80 years of the Hillside Club, Philip Irlam speculated, possibly based on oral evidence, that there was a meeting at a local public house, the Portland Hotel, in 1911 to discuss the formation of a golf club, but ceded that '…the date and the names of those present are unknown.' (Fig.4) He suggested that it was at this meeting that the decision might have been taken to form a golf club and to lease the disused Hill Side Farm golf course.

That such a meeting possibly took place excites further speculation. Birkdale Golf Club had previously rented a dedicated clubroom in the Portland Hotel whilst it was using what an 1895 Ordnance Survey map described as 'Birkdale Golfing Course' on the adjoining Shaw's Hills. After the Club moved to the present Royal Birkdale course in 1897, some of the old course, which extended towards Liverpool Road, was built upon, but, in 1909, six acres were given by the landowner to the Birkdale Urban District Council in exchange for foreshore rights. The land was to be used to create Bedford Park but was left undeveloped until after Birkdale was amalgamated with Southport in 1912. It is possible that after the Birkdale Golf Club abandoned the Shaw's Hill course some neighbouring residents had continued to play informally on surviving remnants of the course and that it was some of these people who came together to form Hillside Golf Club. Although there is no specific evidence to support this hypothesis, the time frame fits and later records show that the early members of Hillside lived largely in this neighbourhood.

As has been demonstrated, precisely how and when the Hillside Golf Club came into being and occupied the Hill Side Farm course is not known. The hard evidence places its foundation somewhere between September 1911 and March 1913. It seems that unless some presently unknown source is found, there is no way of confirming that 1911 is the accurate date, but neither is there any valid reason to challenge the decision of those, including Bert Collinge, who amended the date to 1911 in *The Golfers' Handbook* in 1962.

Fig.4 *Portland Hotel c.1911. Prior to 1897, Birkdale (Royal) Golf Club had a dedicated clubroom in the Portland Hotel, which stood on the corner of Bedford Road and Kew Road adjacent to its Shaw's Hills' course.*

Chapter Two
The Beginnings: Hill Side Farm
1911 - 1923

1911 - 1919

What is known about the Hill Side Farm course? Peter Lloyd would only have had a short lease for his farm from Birkdale's landowner Charles Weld-Blundell, who used such leases as a means of exercising control over his tenants and as a device to retain the flexibility to be able to respond to possible urban development.

Inland from the tall outer sandhills of the dune coast, where star grass struggles to stabilize them and the vegetation cover is not complete, the dune backland becomes completely covered by vegetation. In places sand has been blown inland to form ridges of sandhills across these flatter areas. The local farmers developed special techniques of growing crops on this unpromising land. A feature of the landscape was the small fields, which were known as 'heys', an old English name for enclosures. In the local absence of stone for building walls, banks or 'cops' of earth, which were several feet tall, bounded the fields. In addition to acting as field boundaries, cops also protected the light sandy soil from being carried away by the strong prevailing winds (Fig.5). Hill Side Farm consisted of a mixture of sandhills and rough flatter pastures, on which Lloyd grazed his cattle.

Fig.5 *Hill Side Farm from the S&A course c.1910. The Hill Side farmhouse is in the trees to the right. The terrace of Lloyd's Siding cottages is background left. Note the farm workers on the small cop-surrounded fields of the heys.*

When the railway line from Liverpool to Southport was opened in 1848, it was initially known as the 'Farmers' Line'. Quick to recognise its importance, '...most farmers who were in a position to take shares took as many £5 shares as they could spare money for.' The railway carried fresh milk into the city (In 1897 there were 157 cows in Birkdale producing 600 gallons of milk daily). Early morning loading of milk churns and field produce at Lloyd's Sidings, at the margin of Peter Lloyd's Hill Side Farm, was a daily routine. Liverpool also generated an enormous demand for

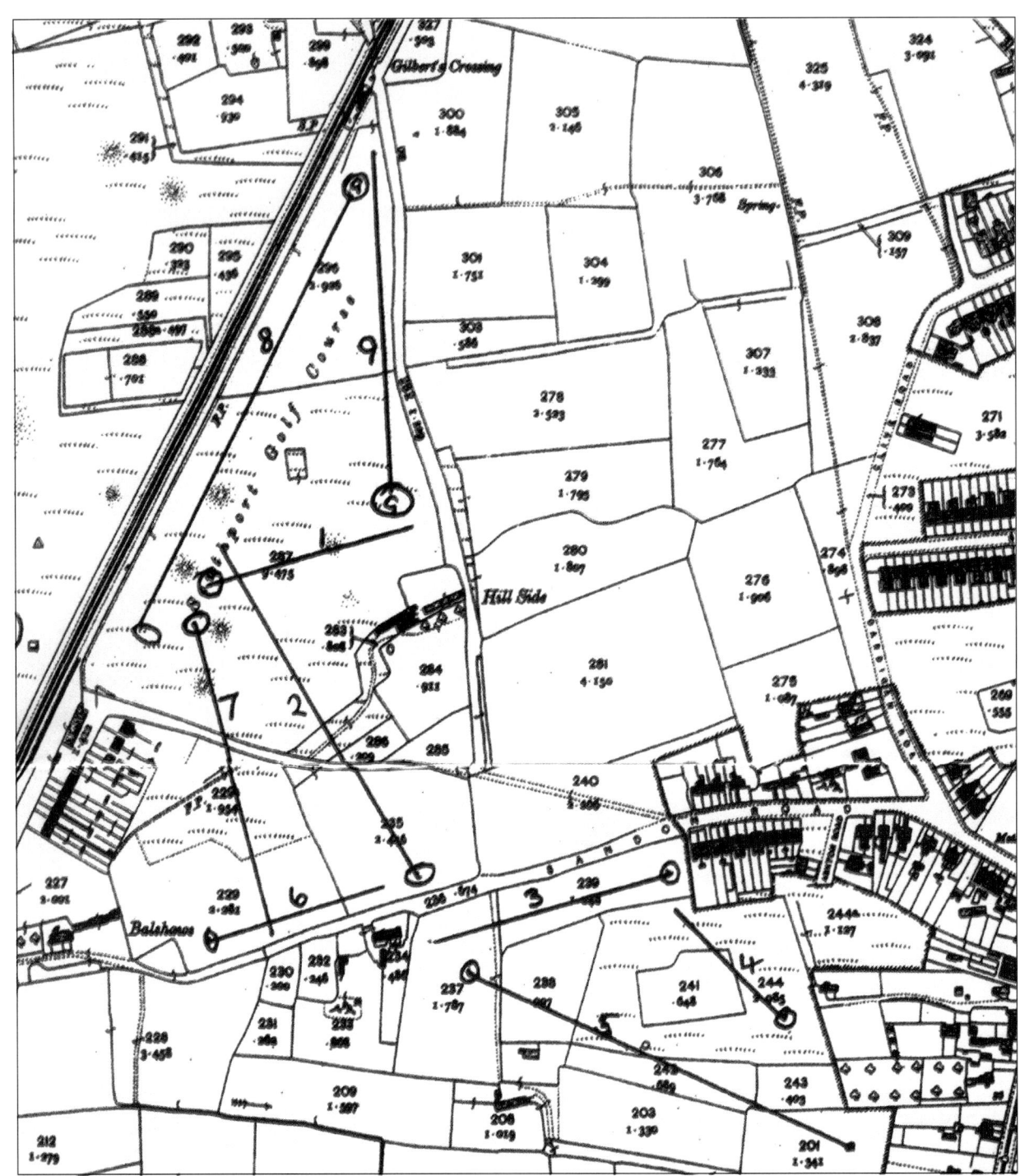

Fig.6 *Hill Side Farm course layout.*
This sketch plan drew on the memories of early members.

animal feed and straw, for the 16,000 horses that were moving goods around the city. More importantly for the future golf clubs, the railway was able to transport vast quantities of manure along with the 'night soil' of the citizens. Thousands of tons arrived annually at Lloyd's Sidings and were used to enrich the thin sandy soil in this area. As early as 1849 a writer in the *Liverpool Mercury* observed that:
'The railway has brought fertility to the fields and the fields within reach of the market.'

There were a number of old tracks in the area and they, along with the field cops, served to determine the irregular layout of the nine-hole course, which Lloyd originally helped to create for the Grosvenor Club. The shortage of space resulted in 'crossings' on several holes (Fig.6). Notes written in 1946 by Walter Child, who had been a founder member of the Grosvenor Club 40 years earlier, gave a limited description of the course. It was, he wrote, '...as rough an outlay as was ever played on.' Flat areas were identified for greens, and once a hole was made it continued to be used. Low fences of stout wooden posts and barbed wire surrounded these small mown/rolled areas, and protected them from grazing cattle. Field cops were utilised as hazards in front of greens and '...were designated as bunkers', thus players had to '...learn to pitch...there could be no running-up.' There was no mention of fairways at this time and the cropping of the grass by cattle was the only attention received by the rest of the ground that made up the nine holes (Fig.7).

Child did describe one of the holes – the 5th. It was the longest on the course, measuring about 400 yards, and was played to a small, elevated green placed in a saucer shaped depression on the top of a conical sandhill. This green was in the hilly south-west corner of the course and was only about 18 feet in diameter and the slope of the hill fell away sharply in all directions. Under hit your approach shot and the ball would roll back, but a strong shot would finish over the green in '...a huge bed of docks, nettles and weeds which grew there in an impenetrable mass.' Such rough also occurred in other areas of the course. In addition to the sandhills, cops and ridges, a further hazard, alongside the 5th hole, was 'Cow Pond.'

Fig.7 *Hill Side Farm course. The cottages on the right are at Lloyd's Siding. Lloyd's farm house is in the trees, background left. Between them lie several holes. This is a rare picture of the original course.*

This was the period when the rubber-cored wound Haskell type of ball was replacing moulded gutta-percha 'gutties', the first having arrived from America in 1901 (Fig.8). Child, who won the first Captain's Prize played on the Hill Side Farm course in 1907, noted that although most of the Grosvenor members used a gutty, he chose to play with a wound ball, but kept a gutty for use on the short holes, because '...it didn't run in the same way.'

The course was 2,850 yards long and was described as '...an ideal sporting sandy course with natural bunkers' in a 1910 publication edited by Harold Hilton, an Open (twice), Amateur (four times), and American Amateur Champion, who was the first stipendiary secretary of the West Lancashire Club and a golf writer.

Fig.8 *Haskell golf balls. Haskell balls arrived in this country from America in 1901 and were expensive. The winner of the Open Championship in 1902 used one.*

The Blundell Club followed the Grosvenor as tenants and by the time that the Hillside Club took over the course there had been minor modifications and its condition might have improved. Peter Lloyd undertook what little attention it received. The 1913-1914, Hillside membership ticket tells us that members were required to '…replace or see replaced any portion of the turf cut out in the act of playing.'

Much of what we know about the infant Hillside Club is derived from this ticket, which contains a copy of the Club's 12 rules. Although located on the Hill Side Farm course, rule one shows the name as 'Hillside Golf Club'. Hillside was the name later adopted for the developing residential district. Ironically it was also the name of a farm in the middle of Hillside's later 18-hole course (see front endpaper). Rule two prescribes that '…the number of members shall not exceed 25.' Such a rule was not unique locally. At its formation in 1884, the rules of Formby Golf Club restricted membership to 'twenty-five residents.' Was this apparently self-imposed limit the reason why, unlike its predecessors on the course, the Hillside Club did not initially seek publicity in the local newspapers in an attempt to attract further members?

On the cover of the ticket the names of the Club's three 'guarantors' are listed. Having this status as early as 1913 suggests that they might have been founder members. The rules show that this trio had the duty to act as a council for the Club. One of them, Fred Jackson the Club's 44-year-old Honorary Secretary/Treasurer, lived at 190 Liverpool Road, midway between the abandoned Birkdale Golfing Course and the Hill Side Farm course (see Fig.3). He worked in the audit office of the Lancashire and Yorkshire Railway and was for 25 years the organist of St John's, the parish church, which was around the corner from his home. He had a reputation as an organiser, who arranged distant trips for the choir and was an active officer in the Southport battalion of the military 'Cadet' movement. Irlam described him as: 'A man of genial disposition.' The other guarantors were 32-year-old bachelor Herbert Wrigley, a hardware dealer, and James Marshall. They too lived in Liverpool Road, near to the course. It appears probable that a group from this area had formed the Club; perhaps there were links with the parish church, and as previously suggested there was also the possibility of a link with the abandoned Birkdale Golfing Course, which was only just over 100 yards from Jackson's home. Despite local enquiries we just do not know.

The previous golfing tenants of Hill Side Farm had erected their pavilions alongside the railway, close to the former Birkdale Station and Gilbert's Crossing. The Hillside Club, however, chose to locate its more modest 'clubhouse' at the inland margin of the course, near to Hill Side Farm. 'Clubhouse' might seem a rather pretentious title for the primitive accommodation provided by a small one-room wooden shed (see Fig.38). The door had a lock and the key was kept at Lloyd's farm.

Although we have no details of the Club's early membership numbers, it appears probable that the restriction to 25 members was soon abandoned. By 1915 the Club is one of a list of seven golf clubs in Southport, which was contained in *Sunny Southport: England's Seaside Garden City*, the Southport Official Guide. The inclusion of this entry suggests that the Club was attempting to attract members and visitors. The entry in this 1915 guide incorrectly gives the Club name as 'Hill Side', as in the name of Peter Lloyd's farm, rather than 'Hillside', as in the Club rules. Another Official Guide - *Southport: A Charming Winter Resort* - was issued by the Corporation in 1916. This states that there were six golf courses in the borough and again lists them. Hillside was not included; did this omission indicate that the Club had lapsed?

From 1916 to 1919 we know nothing of the Club's history. There are no local guidebooks or directories available for these remaining wartime years, the Club has no records for this period and there appears to have been no references to it in the local newspapers. There is a void in the Club's history that does not exist for other Southport clubs during this period.

The First World War would almost certainly have had an adverse impact on a young golf club. After a brief period when it was optimistically believed that the war would be over in a few months, people had to face the grim reality of years of conflict. A proportion of the members would probably have served with the armed forces. It seems highly likely that Hillside would have shared the economic difficulties, which were experienced by all golf clubs, resulting from reduced wartime income.

It is possible that during this period the Club was struggling to survive or was experiencing such hard times that it had closed down. Significantly the names of the three guarantors listed in the 1913-1914 membership ticket, including Fred Jackson, the Honorary Secretary/Treasurer and possible founder of the Club, do not reappear in the Club's later known history, although Jackson continued as the organist at St John's, the nearby parish church, up until his death in 1934. It is another Hillside mystery.

1919 - 1923

From 1919 our knowledge of the Club becomes fuller and interpretation of archive material replaces speculation. The Official Handbook of the Club, which first appeared in 1925, asserted that: 'The present Club has been in existence since 1919.' It was from 1919 that Hillside appears to have adopted many of the practices and characteristics of other golf clubs. It was in this year, shortly after the end of the War, that the Club's first known captain, 53-year-old Richard Mook, was appointed (Fig.9). He lived close to the course in Clinning Road. Directories variously list him as a corn merchant and grocer. His brother, one of a number of local mineral water manufacturers, made 'Mook' a household name in Southport. Richard was to undertake the duties of captain again in 1922, having been president in 1920. He was then to serve as a very active Chairman of Green. In 1925 the Club presented him with a Westminster chiming clock '...in recognition of services rendered.' At the presentation, a speaker referred to him as '...one of the founders of the Club', whilst another described him as '...practically the founder' who had been responsible for its survival. Later in the year his contribution as 'father of the Club' was recognised when he was made its first Honorary Life Member. Oddly no details or dates connected with the Club's foundation were included in reports of these ceremonies.

There is no evidence of any contribution that Mook might have made prior to 1919. Another pioneer in the administration of the Club was George Keeley, a St John's Road resident who was a clerk in the Borough Treasurer's office. After serving in the army during the war, he became secretary of the Club in 1919 and followed Richard Mook as captain in 1920. He also was to be an Honorary Life Member.

It was also about 1919 that 29-year-old Fred Bond was engaged as the Club's first professional. He was a local boy who had been brought up in a cottage attached to Balshaw's Farm, which adjoined Lloyd's Hill Side Farm (see front endpaper). It is probable that he had earlier served as a boy caddie. In addition to his work making and repairing clubs his golfing duties included those of greenkeeper and caddie master. The use of bags to carry clubs was well established by this time and no golfer would dream of carrying his own. Caddies could only be hired through the caddie master and he allocated them, with the golfer having no choice. At the time of the formation of the Hillside Club, local Education Department statistics show that a surprisingly high percentage of boys leaving school in Southport went into the '...blind alley occupation' of full-time caddying. This was a time when the question of Sunday play was very contentious. Hillside shared the compromise agreed by many clubs, that Sunday play was permitted, but that it should be without caddies, so as to allow them to observe the Sabbath. This rule was amended in 1925, when caddies were allowed on a Sunday, but only after midday, thus allowing them to attend church in the morning. By this time new National Insurance regulations, which required boys to have stamps, had sounded the death knell to their employment as full-time caddies. Further confirmation of the use of schoolboys as part-time caddies on Hillside's nine-hole course came in 1988 from Bert Morris, who had undertaken the duties there as a nine-year-old in 1923.

Bond, the professional, was rather patronisingly described to Irlam as '...a glorified caddie who made and mended hickory-shafted clubs.' In fact he was active in the Liverpool and District Golf Alliance, an organisation that was founded about 1919, and which provided the opportunity for professionals and amateurs to come together regularly to play competitive golf. A 1921 report in the Southport Visiter shows that he competed in an Alliance bogey competition at the Liverpool Banking and Insurance Golf Club. (This Club, then Freshfield, lost its course when the land was requisitioned for the RAF's Woodvale airfield, during the Second World War.) Fred was a sufficiently accomplished golfer to be selected to represent the Alliance on several occasions, matches in which he more than held his own.

What do we know about the early members of the Hillside Club? The 1932 handbook suggest that there were about forty members in 1919. Surviving membership tickets for 1921 and 1922 list the members of the committee, whilst newspaper reports, in 1922, yield the results of a monthly competition and the names of the members of a Club team. An analysis of where these members lived resulted in 21 of the 30 names being matched with a street directory address. Of the 21, only one lived outside the immediate neighbourhood of the course; this 'outsider' lived in Southport. None of the members in this sample lived west of the railway line in the socially superior high-class residential suburb - Birkdale Park - the home of the majority of the Birkdale Club's membership. Unlike its two predecessors at Hill Side Farm, the Hillside Club membership appears to have consisted largely of local residents who lived close to the course, around Liverpool Road (see Fig.3). This was the probable explanation for the Hillside Club having its first clubhouse alongside Lloyd's farmhouse, conveniently situated for the east Birkdale homes of its members, rather than alongside the railway, as had been the case with Grosvenor and Blundell clubs, many of whose members lived in Southport or travelled to Birkdale on the train from the Liverpool direction.

Fig.9 Richard Mook, Hillside Golf Club's first captain in 1919.

What kind of backgrounds did the early members have? Although the occupations of only a minority could be identified it did include an architect, a bank manager and head cashier, a builder, a corn merchant, a cotton cloth salesman, a professor of music, a solicitor, an umbrella manufacturer, a window dresser and two railway officials. The Hillside Club membership appears to have been substantially lower middle class (Fig.10).

The rudimentary shed near to the farm would not have provided the clubhouse facilities that the members of the developing club required and a second wooden pavilion was erected in 1920 (Fig.11). This building, which is said to have cost £600, had two rooms, and the Ladies' Section used one of them. The accommodation was insufficient for general meetings

Fig.10 *Clive Road c.1919. These newly built houses were typical of the homes of the early Hillside members. In the middle of the line of three-storey semi-detached villas on the right, were the adjoining homes of the Hargreave and Bon Bernard families, two of the Club's first three lady captains.*

Fig.11 *Hillside Golf Club's second clubhouse 1920.*

and the Club had to hire outside halls for these occasions. The clubhouse had a railed verandah and was erected alongside the railway, making access from Birkdale Station more convenient, an important factor as the membership was progressively drawn from a wider area. Changing the position of the clubhouse resulted in a re-numbering of the holes, the 9th became the 1st, and the 1st became the 2nd and so on.

In addition to his golfing duties Bond was also the Club steward. As such he had charge of the keys for the new pavilion and was responsible for serving members with refreshments. Catering in the clubhouse had been restricted to the sale of mineral water, probably Mook's in earthenware bottles, and bars of chocolate and biscuits. In 1923 the *Southport Visiter* reported a case of a man '…charged with breaking and entering the Hillside Golf House, Dover Road, and stealing eight bars of chocolate.' During the proceedings it was revealed that these goods were displayed on a counter. Board minutes talk of a bar in the pavilion by 1923.

It is plausible to assume that golf competitions were played regularly on the Hill Side Farm course throughout this period. However whilst the other Southport golf clubs made use of local newspapers to report details of their medals, meetings and matches, news of golf at Hillside was seldom published. A report in the *Southport Visiter* in 1922 was an exception and it gave details of the result of a 'monthly button and sweepstake competition'. This unusual title for a competition does not appear in other local golf club calendars, but the prefix of 'monthly' suggests that it might have been a regular feature at Hillside. The scores are given in an orthodox fashion - gross less handicap to give the nett score result. Two of the nine leading players listed had single figure handicaps (four & nine), three were in the teens including Bert Collinge (12) and George Keeley (11), and there were three with handicaps of between 20 and 24.

None of the Club's major competitions and trophies date from the pre-1923 days when the Club played exclusively on the Hill Side Farm course. But it does seem that by 1923 competitive golf at Hillside was getting more organised than might have been the case in earlier times.

The first inter-club fixture in which a Hillside team is known to have participated was at home against the YMCA in 1922. This match, between teams from the town's two youngest golf clubs was handsomely won by Hillside.

Another indication of the Club's growing maturity was when it became a member of the Lancashire Union of Golf Clubs in 1922. Bert Collinge represented it at the Union's 1923 AGM. Collinge was to become an influential administrator within the Club. When neighbouring Birkdale Golf Club hosted the Lancashire Championship in 1923, Hillside offered to extend the courtesy of its course to Birkdale members.

The Ladies

What of the ladies? The Grosvenor Club, which was the first to use this course, had lady 'associate members' from its inception. Unusually, although they paid only a half fee, they were accorded full playing rights. The Blundell Club also had lady associate members. Rule ten on the 1913 Hillside membership ticket included the phrase: '…his or her membership', suggesting that there could be lady members from the time of the Club's foundation.

Contemporary lady golfers wore full ankle length skirts, long-sleeved blouses with stiff collars and frequently a tie, along with a jacket, and a voluminous broad-brimmed hat would top the outfit (Fig.12). The *Southport Visiter* regularly contained an illustrated advertisement advocating the use of 'Ocean Serge' for ladies' golfing outfits. At Hillside, the low fences, which protected the greens from grazing cattle would have contained narrow gaps to allow the long skirted ladies to pass through. Some ladies had leather strips sewn around the bottom of their skirts, both for protection from wear and to hold them down.

J.H. Taylor, the champion who along with Vardon and Braid formed golf's 'Great Triumvirate' and who later became a leading golf course architect, described early ladies' courses as '…little more than putting holes.' The average length of holes on contemporary ladies' courses, such as Lytham and St Annes, was about 150 yards. Some male members condescendingly referred to these short courses as 'hen runs'. Hillside ladies' course would have been achieved by adjusting the position of tees rather than by laying out separate ladies' holes. On occasions, however, the Hillside Ladies' Section sought the Board's permission to play a competition using the men's tees.

The First World War had been a decisive factor in the emancipation of women reflected in the Representation of the Peoples' Act in 1918. Notwithstanding this national progress towards equality, golf clubs largely remained male preserves. What was the position at Hillside? A Ladies' Section

Fig.12 *Local ladies' golfing fashions 1911. The putting green of the West Lancashire Ladies' course. We have no photographs of golfers at the Hill Side Farm course.*

Fig.13 *Mrs Jessie Hargreave, the first captain of the Ladies' Section.*

was officially established at Hillside in 1920, when its first AGM was held. It was at this meeting that 40-year-old Mrs Jessie Hargreave, the wife of a cotton cloth salesman living near to the course in Clive Road, was elected as the first Lady Captain, an office that she was to hold for three years (Fig.13). A Club membership ticket for 1922 gave a prominence to the officers of the Ladies' Section that was not common. Mrs Lodge, whose husband had succeeded Keeley as the Club secretary, was listed as the ladies' secretary. Three of the first six officers of the section were unmarried ladies, demonstrating that membership was not confined to the families of male members. The Board did, however, exercise quite strong oversight of the activities of the Ladies' Section for example its decision that applications for lady membership had to be posted in both clubrooms. It was in 1922 that the Lady Captain's Prize was first contested and it was won by Miss E.A. Lawrenson. The trophy for this competition is the Club's oldest.

Juniors

Although there does not appear to have been any formal recognition of junior players during the early years, the sons and daughters of full members were allowed to play the course, subject to restricted conditions, for which they paid a reduced subscription. Irlam records that Lady Captain Jessie Hargreave's only son, Francis Max, much later recalled playing with Edward Darrah, one of four brothers, who became the Club's outstanding golfer (Fig.14).

Fig.14 *Sandringham School First XI 1917. This private school was in Alexandra Road, Southport. The players seated on the ground were from the left: 14-year-old Denis Chamberlin Darrah and 16-year-old Edward Thompson Darrah, the middle two of four brothers who played at Hillside.*

Chapter Three
The Guardians and the Anxious Years
1923 - 1967

As Southport expanded through its suburbs, the Club faced a future in which the ever-tightening circle of residential property would encroach onto the Hill Side Farm course. Directories show that between 1910 and 1920 some 24 houses were built in Dunkirk, Dunbar, and Kirklees Roads, along with Blundell Drive and Avenue.

An even stronger threat appeared at the southern margin of the course. Under a new Act of Parliament, the Unemployed (Relief Works) Act of 1920, which was legislation intended to create work by promoting public works, the Southport Corporation was going to extend Waterloo New Road south, over a new railway bridge, to link with Liverpool Road close to Windy Harbour Road (Fig.15). Compulsory purchase orders were issued to the landowner in 1921 and the proposed line of the road cut across Hillside's short 6th hole and also interfered with the 3rd, 5th and 7th holes.

Fig.15 *Building the Waterloo New Road railway bridge c.1925. The centre of the roadway coincides with the chimney of the platelayers' hut (Fig.7). The houses of Lloyd's Siding are just visible to the right.*

As the tenant of Peter Lloyd, who leased the farm from Weld-Blundell, the Hillside Club received a compensation payment of £40 from the Corporation. Further south the road and its surrounds led to S&A losing six of its holes and its Liverpool Road clubhouse becoming isolated from the rest of the course (see front endpaper). In addition to the land scheduled to be lost to the Waterloo New Road scheme, the remainder of the Hill Side Farm course would inevitably be engulfed by the tide of bricks and mortar rolling out from Southport. R.H.K. Browning, a national golf journalist, described his 1923 round on the course as '...a wildly adventurous scramble over a region devastée on which the golfers and the road-builders had long ago joined battle.'

There were those within the Hillside membership who recognised the significance of the changes and wanted to investigate the possibility of leasing land for a new course. Hillside was already the smallest and most fragmented of the four nine-hole courses in Southport and some members saw the impending loss of further land as an opportunity for the Club to acquire a new 18-hole course, but there were others who had more modest aspirations. They were satisfied with the existing inexpensive club and thought that proposals for a new course were over-ambitious. The status quo, however, was not a long-term option. As the tenant of Lloyd, the leaseholder, the Club had limited tenure. The progressive agenda won the day and practical steps to obtain a new course were set in motion. Unfortunately the contest between the factions within the Club left scars and there were to be casualties, including some of the pioneers who had made substantial contributions nurturing the Club through its formative years.

In order for a club, which had been accustomed to paying only £8 a year in rent, to finance the leasing of a much larger area of land and to pay for the construction of an 18-hole golf course and a clubhouse, a substantial input of capital was required. To this end a limited liability company was floated. The Hillside Golf Club Limited was founded on the 28th February 1923 with capital of £3,000. The sum was split into 2,250 Ordinary Shares of £1 each and 150 Founders' Shares of £5 each. The holders of Founders' Shares received a commemorative porcelain mug, but more importantly they were entitled to 15 votes per share at company meetings, compared with the single vote per share of the holders of Ordinary Shares. These 1923 company 'founders' should not be confused with the earlier pioneers who originally brought the club into being. Full lady members held two shares but did not qualify for a vote (Fig.16).

The 12 members of the first Board included three of the Club's first four captains and the secretary. The Board's immediate task was to investigate possible ways forward. Approximately 120 members attended the initial Annual General Meeting (AGM) of the limited company, which was held at the Liberal Club in Birkdale in July 1923. One of the directors, R.F. Castleman, took the chair and outlined the progress that had been made. Dissent was in the air and a section of the membership agreed that certain directors on the recently elected Board had already lost their confidence.

An Extraordinary General Meeting (EGM) was hastily convened and, at this August meeting held at the Birkdale Conservative Club, the President, J.E. Hobson, took the chair. In an attempt to heal the wounds opened up at the AGM, a vote of thanks for the work undertaken by the most severely criticised of the directors was carried unanimously. Notwithstanding this gesture three directors resigned from the Board.

Most of the farms in this area were quite small and individually they did not have sufficient land on which to develop an 18-hole course. Consequently, in the search for a site, it was necessary for the Board to deal directly with the Weld-Blundell Estate. George Sherrington, captain in 1923 and 1924 and chairman from 1923 to 1926, was nominated to lead these negotiations on behalf of the Club. Current housing development meant that expansion from the old course was not an option. S&A and the Blundell Club had already taken the other available open plots inland of the railway and the Estate had ambitions to develop the remaining areas for residential purposes. Consequently, Hillside followed the example of Birkdale Golf Club and looked to relocate on the seaward side of the railway. Agreement to lease a strip of approximately 100 acres running south from beyond Waterloo Road, alongside the railway towards Ainsdale, came in November 1923. Much of this land was already leased to four farmers, but as their leases were limited to just one year repossessing the land didn't present difficulties to the landowner. More problematic was the one larger 58-acre plot, Hawes House Farm, which was held on a longer lease by H.W. Roy (See front endpaper). After additional negotiations agreement was reached, and, although there was some reduction in the amount of land attached to it, Hawes House was retained in the middle of the course and Mr Roy became a member of the Club. Weld-Blundell's agent, Mr Walmsley Cotham, who handled the negotiations on behalf of the Estate, was made an honorary member of the Club in recognition of the part that he played in the process.

The decision to lease 105 acres spelt the end of Hillside as a small, cheap neighbourhood club. The new lease was for 21 years and the Club faced the necessity of paying £63 15s (£63.75p) per annum for the first eight years and thereafter the annual figure increased to £175 15s (£175.75p).

Course construction was carried out by Conway of Halifax, a fertiliser manufacturer and dealer, and work started in January 1923, some ten months before the lease was finally signed. Such administrative tardiness was characteristic of the management of the Weld-Blundell Estate. Conway employed a force of approximately 40 men. Turf for the tees and greens

Fig.16 *A lady's share certificate 1945.
This was issued to Mabel Francis and was signed by three
of the most influential officials in the history of Hillside Golf Club.*

was obtained from a farm in Ainsdale. During this construction stage the Club employed an additional horse and man for 14sh (70p) a day. By August ten holes of the new course were linked to eight on the old to give a temporary 18-hole layout. After an initial payment of £600 the Club was committed to pay Conway the remainder of the £2,590 in instalments. By April 1924 the contractor's work was complete and the 18-hole course was officially opened. Several of the new tees and greens did not stand up to the wear and tear of golf and had to be replaced. The Club's relationship with the contractor had become strained and solicitors became involved as the dispute rumbled on for several years.

The Board decided against moving the wooden clubhouse to the new course and sought estimates for a new clubhouse designed by Herbert Archer, an architect and Board member, who supervised the commissioning and building process. Following common golf club practice he designed the clubhouse in such a way that, if necessary, it could be sold as a house.

Land for the clubhouse was leased separately from the course as the mortgage required the security of a longer lease. A double plot, on what was to become Hastings Road, was obtained on a three nines (999-years) lease, when most local leases were confined to two nines (99-years). The tender for building the clubhouse, accepted at the EGM of November 1923, was for £2,624 and was from J.G. Wilkinson, a member and a mayor of Southport. The building was to be financed by personal loans carrying five per cent interest. Two of the larger loans came from Peter Lloyd the leaseholder of Hill Side Farm (£200) and Wilkinson, the builder, who offered to delay the payment of £250; both appear to have a commercial motive in the Club relocating. The decision to build the new clubhouse was finally taken on Saturday 19th December 1924. During the building period, the pavilion on the old nine-hole course was used, and its later sale, to St. Andrew's Lawn Tennis Club, raised £100.

The tenancy agreement with Peter Lloyd for the Hill Side Farm course was terminated in December 1924, but the Club continued to pay him the rent for a further two years and in 1925, despite the financial problems it faced, his loan was repaid and he resigned his membership. The short period during which Lloyd's small course had played such a significant part in the development of golf in Southport had passed and house builders quickly moved in (Fig.17).

It seems that the membership of the Club was ill prepared to face its new financial obligations. The Club had moved out of the comfort zone where it declared a profit of £27 on a modest turnover in 1924, to a loss of £405 in 1925. There were liabilities in the form of a bank overdraft of £541, a balance of £1,550 owing on the building of the course, whilst the loan debt to members stood at £1,286. There was an urgent need to secure additional income. The most obvious potential source was through an increase in the number of members and it was decided to accept a further 40. Advertisements were placed in local newspapers and an inducement offered to new members in the form of waiving an entrance fee. Candidates were required to have a handicap, but oddly this requirement could be ignored by payment of an entrance fee. The offer of 40 places was quickly taken up. An official club handbook, a popular contemporary publicity device, was produced for the first time in 1925 (Fig.18). In an attempt to further boost membership amalgamation overtures were made to the successful Blundell Club, the former tenant of the Hill Side Farm course that had moved to a nine-hole course at Ainsdale. After meetings between the officials of the two clubs, Hillside met the same negative response that had greeted a similar approach earlier made to the Blundell Club by S&A, when it was experiencing financial problems.

Lottery schemes and one-off money raising events could never meet the Club's financial needs. Shares in the Club were hawked around the neighbourhood on a door-to-door basis, and the Board successfully sought to ask the founder members to call up unpaid capital amounting to £350. More controversially an increase in the annual subscriptions was proposed. The proposal was for the ladies' fees to be raised from £2 2s (£2.10p) to £3 and in the case of men from £3 to £4 14s 6d (£4.72p). When this was rejected at an EGM, held on the 10th May 1926, the directors felt obliged to resign en bloc, as did the Captain, C.H. Taylor. They did offer to prepare a balance sheet to be handed over to a new Board, and George Sherrington, C.H. Taylor, and J.E. Hobson were nominated as interim managers.

The Club was struggling to find a satisfactory solution to its management hiatus, when a relatively new member, Louis Rowlandson, a manager with the LMS Railway Company, was elected to chair a further EGM held on the 4th June, which had been called to consider the resignation of the directors, and the finances of the Company. Rescue schemes were discussed and it was agreed that they should be submitted to a new Board of Directors. At an AGM held later in June,

Fig.17 *Builders take over the former Hill Side Farm course c.1932.*

Fig.18 *The first club handbook 1925. The publisher used this art deco cover on a number of contemporary club handbooks.*

Rowlandson was elected chairman of the Club, a position this strong authoritarian character was to hold for 14 years (Fig.19). He received sterling support from Hugh Davies, a retired civil servant who had been an active member for several years. Davies joined the new Board in 1926, and in the following year resigned this position to become the Club's honorary secretary, a post he was to hold for 24 years. Irlam describes him as '...something of a martinet'; he was certainly an imposing figure who helped Rowlandson to provide the financial stability the Club needed in order to survive.

annual dinner at the Prince of Wales Hotel. A convivial evening was enjoyed with several good friends and apparently he had quite a lot to drink. Rowlandson heard about this and, believing that Darrah had let down the image of the Hillside Club, gave him '...a dressing down.' Darrah told him to '...go to blazes' as he was not dealing with his railway people and never spoke to him again. He resigned from Hillside and joined Birkdale in 1933. His photograph subsequently disappeared from the portrait gallery of past captains, we know not when, but can perhaps surmise why. The gap has now been filled by a digitally

Fig.19 *Entertaining the Captain, C. Hodkinson, in 1947. This group includes most of the men who led the Club through its financially anxious years. From the left: L.F. Rowlandson, J. Carson, W.R.H. Gibbs, H.S. Collinge, J.M.T. Reynolds, C. Hodkinson, B. Turner, A. Poirrette, A. Crampton, G. Dixon, J.A.W. Hepburn and H. Davies.*

Rowlandson's 'imperial' style was demonstrated with his dealing with one of the Club's captains. The 1926 captain was Arnold Darrah. He was the eldest of the four Darrah brothers and a seven-handicap golfer. He lived in then fashionable Scarisbrick Street in the Southport town centre, and, at the age of only 26, he was the youngest member to be appointed captain. It was, he recalls, a position with very little power, because executive responsibility lay with the Chairman and the Board - 'They' he said '...made all the decisions'. Darrah was invited by the Captain of Birkdale to attend that club's

assembled 'red jacket' image, which includes the face of a more mature Darrah.

The new Board proposed the increase in membership fees that had been rejected at the meeting held in the previous month. After discussion, this resolution was passed by the founder members and the ordinary members at a series of meetings held in July 1926. The club trustees had also asked to be relieved of their responsibilities, which passed to the new Board.

The financial crisis was not quickly resolved and in 1927 creditors were pressing and a receiver was appointed. At yet another EGM in May 1927 Louis Rowlandson was able to point to '...a silver lining beyond the storm clouds.' Original loan holders agreed to leave their money on loan, interest free, for a minimum of three years. This was coupled to a scheme of full repayment of the principal sum over a period of ten or 12 years. Members also agreed to make additional loans of £5 or more each, which would attract interest of five per cent, with no interest to be payable for three years. Just under a £1,000 was raised and this was sufficient to liquidate all capital liabilities, with the exception of the course contractor. Conway agreed to defer payment of the principal until the Club became financially sound, and accepted six per cent interest on the outstanding balance. Repayments were started in 1929.

The 'rescue' package eventually bore fruit, although in 1930 the Board had to ask loan holders to forego interest payments for a further three years. By 1932 the Club was able to start these repayments.

The transition of the Club to its new status had not been effected without further casualties. Former stalwarts of the infant club, George Sherrington and Herbert Archer, resigned in 1928, as did former secretary George Keeley when his honorary life membership was rather shabbily withdrawn in 1931, along with that of Richard Mook, the Club's first captain. Keeley, '...saddened by the experience', was to join S&A. The Club's honours board and gallery of past captains' portraits continued to ignore those who held office before the company was established in 1923. It was only in 2009 that the honours board was amended to include those who had been captain between 1919 and 1923. We should not be surprised, perhaps, that 1923 was adopted in some instances as the year of the Club's foundation.

Whilst the Club was experiencing its financial turmoil, the Southport Corporation had produced a new town-planning scheme. Following a public enquiry in 1927, Hillside's new course, along with that of its neighbour Birkdale Golf Club, was included in dune land that was designated as 'pleasure

Fig.20 *A Weld-Blundell Estate plan 1914.*
This plan shows projected residential development across what became Hillside Golf Club course.

grounds and open space', thus losing its value to the landowner as an area for potential residential development (Fig.20). Following the death, in 1927, of Birkdale's landowner Charles Weld-Blundell without a direct male heir, the property passed to relatives and was administered by what had become the Ince-Blundell Estate. Many local estates were selling off land at this time and, as the town-planning scheme had dramatically reduced the potential value of this section of dune land, the Corporation stepped in and, in 1928, bought 750 acres between Waterloo Road and Shore Road Ainsdale, including the freehold of the Hillside and Birkdale courses. It seems that, in addition to preserving an open space and providing a sporting amenity for residents, the Corporation was looking to golf as a way of attracting visitors to the town. Hillside Golf Club had a new landlord, one who was more sympathetic to the concerns of golf clubs than the Estate had been.

A new lease for the course was negotiated with the Corporation in 1931 for a period of 30 years at an annual rent of £175 15s (£175.75p). Hillside's neighbour Birkdale Golf Club was given an 99-year lease, but had to pay an additional £100 per annum rent, bringing the total to £350, and was required to spend at least £10,000 in the next seven years on producing a championship standard course with a clubhouse to match. The plans for this work had to meet the approval of the authority. Similar requirements were placed on the 99-year lease of the Hesketh Club, whose course was purchased by the Corporation from the Hesketh Estate. The Corporation, which wanted to promote tournament golf in the town, was apparently cognisant of Hillside's strained financial position. It received a much shorter lease than the other two tenants, but the authority did not impose additional burdens on the Club, which was still struggling to pay for its recently laid out course and new clubhouse. The new landowner did, however, exercise a degree of oversight, for example the Corporation insisted that the list of green fees to be charged should be submitted to it for approval and that a belt of coniferous trees be planted to protect the course and residential building further inland from blown sand.

A 1932 Southport Corporation guide book shows that Hillside, although now an 18-hole course, still charged green fees at the same level as Southport's three nine-hole courses, much less than those charged by the town's other three clubs with 18-hole courses. An unusual feature was the offer of a reduced summer green fee after 5.30pm.

Hillside's financial crises had coincided with the years of the Great Depression. As this period passed the financial recovery continued. By 1932 the accounts were recording a nett profit, and confidence was such that a £662 scheme to improve the clubhouse facilities was undertaken, funded by an increased mortgage on the building. Between 1927 and 1940 a gross revenue loss of £369 was transformed into a gross profit of £852, whilst liabilities were reduced from £4,300 to £106.

The Club was fortunate in having strong successors to follow Rowlandson as chairman of the Board during this period of consolidation. In 1940 Arnold Poirrette took over. He had been captain in 1932 and had served on a number of committees. Irlam judges him to have been '…a very good chairman, tough but willing to listen'. Poirette was also prepared to make interest free loans to the Club when required.

With the country again involved in a World War, life at Hillside took on a completely different aspect from 1939. Absent members serving in the armed forces were granted membership without the payment of fees. The golfing programme was severely restricted; the finances suffered and the Club was obliged to remortgage the clubhouse in 1940; but after hostilities ceased the Club was able to recover.

Bert Collinge followed Poirrette as chairman in 1953. His administrative contributions stretched back to the days of the nine-hole course. He was captain in 1931 and again over 30 years later in 1962. He was a member of the Board from 1934, serving on the House and Green Committees. Irlam's verdict on Collinge was that he '…didn't suffer fools gladly and became more authoritarian over the years.' In addition to overseeing dramatic reconstruction of the course, a £2,628 scheme of clubhouse improvements was implemented. His service to the Club resulted in the award of a richly deserved Honorary Life Membership in 1960. In 1986, the **H.S. Collinge Trophy** was inaugurated in his memory.

The strong, authoritarian leadership exercised by the long-serving chairmen, Rowlandson, Poirrette and Collinge, didn't always win friends, but it helped to steer Hillside from its modest and rather precarious status in 1923, through a period of financial turmoil, to becoming one of the region's leading golf clubs. The nature of points raised from the floor at AGMs suggest that members sometimes felt excluded from the decision making process by the dictatorial management style employed by this trio.

Chapter Four
A New Course and Clubhouse 1923-1967

The Course

The land leased for the course in November 1923 was just over 105 acres. It was a long relatively narrow strip running alongside the seaward flank of the railway from south of Waterloo Road to Ainsdale, interrupted by Hawes House. Hawes was the old local name for sandhills. Unlike the Hill Side Farm course, this course extended up to and just into the margins of the tall sandhills. The conditions of the lease included the requirement that the sandhills should be kept grassed to prevent the sand blowing. The Weld-Blundell Estate had long insisted on tenants planting deep-rooted marram, locally called star grass, to bind the sandhills. Sea buckthorn and dwarf willow scrub also grew abundantly on the tall dunes. Bernard Darwin described similar rough on the adjacent Birkdale links as '…a most devilish and tenacious hazard.' For several hundred years the sandhills (Hawes) had been used as warrens for the farming of rabbits (see front endpaper). Despite repeated attempts by greenkeepers to control them, their descendants are still a nuisance on the golf courses along this coast (Fig.21).

Using sandhills would have made the fashioning of a golf course an expensive exercise; consequently only a small area of the taller dunes was included in the lease with the major part of the course being laid out on the relatively flatter dune backland alongside the railway. Browning described it as '…an undulating valley of turf in which the natural features are few.' Much of this land had been cultivated, if only as pasture, and required little in the way of preparation (See front endpaper). In line with the estate policy thousands of pine trees were planted along the margin of the golf course, at the edge of the tall sand dunes, in order to provide protection from the inland incursion of blown sand.

Fig.21 *Shooting rabbits on Hawes Farm c.1910. The keepers would have used the bagged ferrets to flush rabbits out of their burrows. Note the relatively flat heath land with the tall sandhills ('Rabbit Warrens') in the background.*

Conway, the course constructor, was also the course architect. Hillside was believed to have been this company's first golf course commission and Irlam suggests that Bert Collinge was '...influential in the design.' The 1925 handbook included a copy of the card, which showed the course as being 6011 yards long, with the two longest holes measuring 478 yards, but only one other over 400 yards (See rear endpaper).

The 1st hole, with its drive threatened by its proximity to the railway, is one of only four holes that now survive in anything approaching their form on this original course. The 2nd, 3rd and 4th holes formed a now vanished loop to the right of the 1st green, whilst the 5th was largely the present 2nd (Fig.22). Browning thought that the excellence of the first five holes owed more to the skills of the course designer than to nature. The presence of field cops demonstrated that much of the course was laid out on former agricultural land and they were particularly evident from the elevated tee of the short 6th hole (Fig.23). Although the field cops have been largely removed from the course over the years, remnants still remain, for example alongside the track to the right of the 1st fairway and between the 9th tee and the fairway.

Another original hole, the shape of which can still be recognised was the 7th (the present 5th), with its green in the corner formed by the railway and Hawes House. The approach to the green was guarded by two pot bunkers set in a coll between two hills (Fig.24). Having played this hole, golfers would follow the path between the railway and Hawes House around to the 'detached', now vanished, southern section of the course (See rear endpaper). Browning thought that the 6th and 7th holes, which made use of natural features, were '...particularly good holes.'

Beyond Hawes House were the parallel 8th, 9th and 10th holes on former Hawes House Farm land (Fig.25). Browning charges that these three holes '...cannot wholly escape the criticism of being laid up and down a flat field.' Shallow demarcation trenches dug between the holes served to mark internal out-of-bounds. The return north was via the short 11th hole (Fig.26); this 156 yard long hole was the course's only venture into the tall dunes. Its narrow green set in a 'wilderness of sandhills' had steep slopes on either side and the entrance was flanked with deep bunkers. Being a short hole, the expense of creating a fairway was saved. Having come down from the hills, behind Hawes House, the round proceeded through the 12th, 13th and 14th, a second trio of roughly parallel, relatively flat holes.

Fig.22 *The 5th (now 2nd) green. The view back to the clubhouse over flat former agricultural land. The tee was alongside the railway and on the left is the 4th fairway leading to the green, which was behind the 1st green. The path behind the 5th green leads to the 6th tee on top of the tall sandhill that still backs the 2nd green.*

The Club's 1932 handbook contains a description of the course by R. Endersby Howard. He was enchanted by what he describes as its:

...naturalness...the dunes, the sand pits, the woods and the gently rolling contour of the ground, were there waiting for someone to come along and stake out places for teeing grounds and putting greens. Designing it and constructing it must have been a joy.

He identifies as '...a worthy example of this blessedness' the 14th hole. (This hole has now been split between the present 6th and 7th holes.)

Fig.23 The 190 yard long 6th hole. The exposed tee was on the hill behind the present 2nd green. Field cops had been left around this hole and formed what was known as the 'paddock', short of the green on the right.

Fig.24 Pot bunkers in front of 7th (now the 5th) green. These were later rebuilt as a single large bunker with a railway sleeper face, making it a blind shot from the fairway to the green.

Fig.25 *Potato picking on Hawes Farm. The electric train dates the photograph as being after 1904. This area of cultivated ground alongside the railway was flat.*

Fig.26 *The green of the short 11th hole. It was the only hole that was up in the sand dunes. Down to the right are the flatter 8th and 9th holes.*

Its length is 431 yards, it teems with problems, and yet not a single hazard has been made for it. From a raised teeing ground, at the back of which is a range of fir trees the player aims to place his drive between two sandhills. His second shot has to carry a low ridge of dunes. On either side are sand pits of a rugged grandeur such as the constructed bunker never quite attains. The putting green has the touch of a fairy land. At the back is a large sandhill, and immediately on the right is an old thatched cottage so bounteously surrounded by trees that only peeps of it can be obtained here and there (Fig. 27).

Although the short 17th hole, which was on a line to the left of the present 10th, was deemed the 'easiest' on the card, the 185 yard drive into the prevailing wind, to a well bunkered green in front of the pine-clad dunes, was a tough one (Fig.28). Browning thought that it was a superlative hole. He was also impressed by the 15th, 16th and 18th holes '...all good two-shot holes, with the sand-hills' that formed the course boundary, '...breaking into the fairway on our hooking hand.'

Howard also noted the '…variety of stances which it (the course) provides.' Such gentle undulations were then judged to represent golfing excellence and in this respect he compared Hillside with Hoylake. Browning perhaps offered a more impartial view and concluded that the course was '...very definitely laid out with an eye to a less exacting standard of play than, say, Birkdale.' He perhaps missed the point that the expense of creating a course in taller wild dune country would also have been too expensive for Hillside at this time.

In October 1923, Bygate, the greenkeeper, was dismissed and James Dutton, one of the four displaced farmers whose land had been used to make the course, was appointed as head greenkeeper. He and his family lived in the former Hillside Farm cottage, which can still be seen alongside the 7th green. His wage was £2 12s 6d (£2.62p) per week and his wife was permitted to sell mineral water to golfers and staff. The need for economies later led to a reduction of 5s (25p) a week in Dutton's wage, and 2s 6d (12.5p) from the other men. It appears that Dutton experienced difficulties in supervising his men. He complained to the Board that the men were not doing what they were told. It seems that they were even spending time catching rabbits during working hours. Although retained, Dutton was relieved of the title of head greenkeeper and these duties were temporarily passed to the secretary.

Fig.27 *Hillside Farm alongside the 14th (present 7th) green. There is '...an old thatched cottage so bounteously surrounded by trees that only peeps of it can be obtained.' Bill Gibbs, the golfer, was captain in 1933.*

The claim in the 1932 handbook that: 'The services of a first-class golf architect were obtained' appears to refer to advice received in October 1927. It came from T.J. Renouf, the professional from the Hopwood Club in north Manchester (Fig.29). After his visit to Hillside he produced plans for major modifications to the links. This advice had come at no cost to the Club as the Captain Jesse Reynolds, a man who was to be captain on four further occasions, had met Renouf's expenses. Constrained by the Club's financial problems, full and immediate implementation of Renouf's recommendations was not possible but some improvements, particularly in relation to vital drainage on the lower lying 1st, 2nd, 4th and 5th fairways were made in addition to shaping the 1st and 3rd greens. By 1932 technological improvement in the form of the newly introduced steel-shafted clubs was dictating the need to lengthen golf courses and over 300 yards had been added to Hillside.

Fig.28 The short 17th hole. Followed the line of the present 10th hole, but the green was short of the conifer-clad tall dunes.

Fig.29 An exhibition match for wartime charity at S&A, 1917. The four professionals holding clubs were from the left: J.H. Taylor, Ted Ray, James Braid, and T.G. Renouf.

Alterations that had been made to the course had been achieved with the Club's own staff. Course maintenance had been by manpower and horse-drawn implements, including mowers and rollers. Regular rolling appears to have formed a major part of contemporary greenkeeping practice. By 1923 a Dennis motor mower had been obtained and T.C. Macauley, an automobile engineer, who was a low handicap golfer and a 'founder' member of the Club, maintained it. A new shed to house it was built at a cost of two pounds. More equipment was gradually acquired. For example in 1923 a second-hand roller was bought at auction, in 1926 the ladies paid for the purchase of a 12 inch hand mower, and in 1939 one member paid £76 for two auto scythes. Greenkeeping was a labour intensive activity; a woman and a boy were employed to undertake the task of weed control of the greens by hand. Will Bond took over as head greenkeeper, although the cottage was occupied up until 1957 by Foster, one of his men. The area of the cottage was then used to house chickens.

Hawes House and its remaining land, in the middle of the course, were offered for sale to the Corporation in 1936. Although the whole property was declined, Hillside did obtain a strip of new land to the north of the house, which enabled a number of course improvements to be made. The major one was the removal of the short 3rd hole, from the loop, and the construction of a new short 7th hole on the land acquired from Hawes House. This plot consisted of a patch of meadowland '...on which Boy Scouts camped annually', which was surrounded by woodlands. The present 6th tee has been extended back into what was the approach to this 160 yards long 7th hole. It was set in an amphitheatre of trees, and posed the threat of going out of bounds with the railway to the left of the green and Hawes House boundary on the right (Fig.30). Problems didn't finish there, the green was a rising plateau pear shape with bunkers closing the entrance and carrying round each side. Having played this demanding hole golfers would follow the path between Hawes House and the railway to the 8th tee. Further course changes included work on the 8th and 9th fairways to give them a dog-leg shape and building a new green for the 8th in the dunes. Work on the short 11th included cutting a new tee into a sand dune to give it some protection from the prevailing wind.

Fig.30 *The short 7th hole which replaced the 3rd. It was described as one of the most picturesque short holes in Southport.*

World War Two put any prospect of further course development onto the back burner. After much of mainland Europe fell to the Panzer blitzkrieg, the German army stood on the Channel coast poised ready for invasion. As part of the preparation to repel possible airborne glider attack, obstacles to landing were erected on open flat spaces. At Hillside these took the form of steel hawsers suspended eight foot high, on heavy timber supports. The minutes of the AGM held in August 1940 described them as 'Aero-Traps'. These were provided by Club member, J.L. Crawford, on the 6th, 8th, 9th, 10th, 12th, 13th and 14th fairways. They caused less long-term damage than was the case on other local courses where trenches were dug.

The Hillside course did suffer from enemy action. Southport did not experience the sustained aerial bombardment inflicted on Liverpool and Bootle. Bombing was limited to odd incidents, mainly cases of aircraft returning after raiding

Merseyside and jettisoning the remains of their bomb loads prior to following their escape flight path, up the Ribble valley and across the Pennines to the North Sea. In the spring of 1941, landmines and a stick of incendiary bombs fell across the 8th, 9th and 10th fairways, south of Hawes House, and the craters remained for a number of years.

To maintain the upkeep of the course, the professional John Burton took on supervisory duties in 1940. When he left the Club in 1942 to work as a haulage contractor and eventually to serve in the RAF, responsibility for work on the course passed to Bert Collinge. The greenkeeping staff was down to two; Will Bond, who served from 1919 to 1946, and his brother Fred, the former professional, who worked on the course throughout the war. Neither of them could drive the tractor and members helped with course maintenance. The fertilisers normally used were not available and, overall, the reduction in the expense of maintaining the course helped to balance the books during the war years.

There was pressure to help in food production and, as part of the Club's war effort, sheep were allowed to graze on the course. This reduced the grass-cutting burden, but, as in the Club's early days on the Hill Side Farm course, protective fencing had to be put around the greens. A new local rule stated that: 'A ball lying in a hole or a scrape made by a sheep in a bunker may be lifted out and placed without penalty.' The Club also had an allotment for growing vegetables. It was situated close to the old 3rd green and was still producing vegetables for the dining room in the 1950s, before it became a turf nursery.

A post-war increase in membership caused the course to be congested and thoughts were turning to course reconstruction. The lack of two convenient starting points close to the clubhouse was highlighted by the growing practice of some members to drive their cars to the Ainsdale end of the course, beyond Hawes House, and start from the 10th tee. The clubhouse was their halfway house to which they returned when they had completed 18 holes (Fig.31). J.A. Steer, the professional at Lytham Green Drive, who had a regional portfolio of planning golf construction work, produced a new plan and Hillside professional John Burton subsequently suggested further modifications, but post-war austerity and the delay in agreeing the boundary details of a new lease with the Corporation meant that neither scheme was implemented. Encouraged by the landowner, the Corporation, tree planting continued. A further 2,000 pines were planted between Hawes House and the 8th hole in 1948. Course improvements were confined to a new putting green opened in 1952. Nevertheless, there was still energy within the Club, principally Harold Greenwood, Chairman of the Green Committee, and Bert Collinge, the Chairman of the Board, driving the reconstruction bandwagon forward.

By December 1953 serious consideration was being given to altering the 15th and 18th holes. The fact that the course was to be used for the final qualifying rounds for Royal Birkdale's first Open Championship in the following year led to a delay in implementation. The Club's near neighbour had received its Royal designation in 1951.

Major reconstruction work at Hillside was enabled to proceed as a result of a novel scheme worked out with the Southport Corporation, the Club's landlord. The agreement was based on the cost of construction being offset by the sale of sand for use in industry. The work was to be undertaken by a subcontractor- John Livesey Ltd - under the direction of the Borough Engineer with Ephraim Patrick, Southport's Superintendent of Parks, being the link man on the ground. Work began in 1955 on the 15th hole, now the 8th. Sandhills to the left of this hole, which then constituted the course boundary, were extensively excavated to create a sharply dog-legged fairway, which was opened for play in April 1957. The 18th, which was played from an elevated tee at the margin of the dunes, had 68 yards added to its length, the fairway was moved to the seaward as a result of a strip of land being granted by the Corporation at no additional cost and hills were excavated to accommodate the fairway, and the new green was sited in the centre of the old practice putting green. This hole was opened for play in December 1959.

From 1956 the Club had confidential exploratory talks with representatives of the local authority about the possibility of a major revision of the course. After receiving a favourable reception, the Hillside Board formally wrote to the Corporation in 1957 to investigate the possibility of the Club exchanging the southern 'detached' portion of its course beyond Hawes House for the area of tall wild dunes that lay between the Hillside and Royal Birkdale courses (Fig.32). These dunes were some of the largest on the south-west Lancashire coast. The land the Club wished to surrender was that of the 8th, 9th, 10th and 11th holes. It was the land furthest away from the clubhouse and included holes, which were, according to golf journalist Tom Scott, '...by common consent...the poorest golf holes.' Fortuitously this was land that was attractive to the

Fig.31 *An aerial view of the course 1961. © Crown Copyright. All Rights Reserved. Sefton Licence No. 1000181922010. See course plans (rear endpaper) for hole numbers.*

Fig.32 *Walking the wild tall dunes. The clubhouse can be seen at the right-hand edge of the photograph.*

Corporation; it stood close to Ainsdale Station and the village, and part of it was subsequently used as the site for now defunct Ainsdale (Hope) High School. Revenue from the sale of the sand that was extracted during the course reconstruction was to be used to pay for the building of new holes. Fred W. Hawtree, one of the country's leading golf course architects, whose portfolio included work on the Royal Birkdale and Royal Liverpool links, was commissioned by the Club to design a course on this basis. In 1958 he submitted detailed plans that satisfied the Club's course requirements and provided sufficient data to allow the Corporation to calculate precisely the volume of sand that there would be available for sale. The Corporation was well satisfied and an agreement was quickly reached.

Central to the Club's design brief was that the course should consist of two loops of nine holes each starting at or near the clubhouse and Hawtree's plan, which involved a major reordering of the 1923 course, fulfilled this requirement. He also gave advice on the construction of the 15th (now the 8th) and 18th holes that was already in progress. In 1960, work began on what are now the 16th and 17th holes and in 1961 on the 11th (Figs.33 & 34). A massive removal of sand was at the heart of Hawtree's plan to design monumental valleys through which he threaded the isolated fairways of Hillside's back nine (Fig.35). The sub-contractor for this phase was William Rainford of Liverpool. The newly shaped fairways were of yellow sand which provided no kind of a base for the growing of turf. The received greenkeeping wisdom was to enrich the sand as much as possible in order to encourage growth. Thousands of tons of topsoil, peat moss, manure and sewage sludge were incorporated before the fairways were seeded. The resulting surfaces were such that John Beherend, writing of the Amateur Championship at Hillside in 1979, described the fairways as '...softer than one normally associates with links golf.'

Legend has it that an old car was buried under the new 17th fairway. Some suggest that a hollow created by the collapse of its rusted and rotted body shell now marks the location. Although the reconstruction was so extensive, it was managed in such a way that members were able to continue to play on the course. Nevertheless, it was only after several seasons, during which players had to play first from the margins of the new fairways and later to tee up, that the new surfaces were fit for play. Fortunately the Club had a dedicated and skilful head greenkeeper, Ted MacAvoy who had been appointed in 1947, and was a member of a well-known family of local greenkeepers, having formerly been on the staff at the West Lancashire Club.

Some minor work had been done on the holes in the first half. In 1960 professional John Burton re-designed the 7th green, supervised its construction by the Club staff and achieved a hole in one on the first occasion on which he played it. Initially this short hole was played from a tee to the west of the 6th green, but this was later replaced by a tee cut into a sand dune to its east (See rear endpaper). In December 1963 plans submitted by Hawtree for the front nine holes were agreed, with some amendments. Changes to the plan continued to be accepted whilst construction was in progress. Eric Hawkins suggested the creation of a deep-water hazard near to the new 3rd green. The surrounding area was relatively flat and spoil from the pond was used to create a bank at the back of the green and to build up the nearby 2nd fairway. This work was completed in 1967 and for the purpose of this book is taken to be the end of this reconstruction.

From the time when the Corporation became the landowner, it had been concerned to maintain the pine tree planting programme at Hillside. The Club was buying in thousands of two-year-old seedlings, rearing them in nursery beds for a further two years before planting them out, but the failure rate was so high that it was eventually decided to buy fewer better trees. The Corporation's control of this facet of managemen was demonstrated by the fact that the Club

Fig.33 *11th and 17th fairways 1989. This photograph gives some impression of the height of the surrounding sand dunes.*

Fig.34 *The short 16th hole 1989. Beyond the course boundary alongside the 16th hole is a 'sea' of wild sand dunes. Located in an excavated hollow, the hog-backed, stepped green is set obliquely to the line of the hole.*

was not even allowed to thin out the trees without permission. The belt of pine trees that had been planted in the sandhills marking the margin of the old course became a central spine running through the course. Much of the earlier planting had been on the exposed holes to the south of Hawes House.

Chairman of Green, Harold Greenwood, who had been very involved in the course reconstruction project, died in 1962; thereafter Bert Collinge, the Club chairman took on the leading role. His period as chairman came to an end in 1967, but he briefly continued as Chairman of Green. His relationships, with the Southport Corporation and within the Club, particularly with the Green Committee, were not always harmonious. But he saw the Club through a critical period to a position where it enjoyed a links course of the highest quality.

Writing in 1968, Tom Scott reported that many people had told him '...that here were the finest second nine holes in the whole length and breadth of England.' He went on to say '...you can take my word for it that Hillside's second nine are of very great quality.'

Fig.35 *Aerial view of the north end of the course.*
It illustrates how the holes of Hillside's back nine were carved out of the tall sand dunes.

Hillside Artisans: 'To be, or not to be?'

Caddying had introduced golf to a wider social audience and, not surprisingly, had created an appetite for playing the game. One way in which working-class men were able to participate in golf was as 'artisans'. Artisans enjoyed limited free, or very cheap, golf in return for duties undertaken on the golf course.

The Artisan Golfers' Association was formed in 1921. Such was the national impact of artisan golf, that in 1929, an artisan won the English Amateur Championship. The first Southport club to have an artisan section was Birkdale in 1931. An entry in the Hillside Board minute book in 1936 reveals a suggestion that an artisan section should be formed at Hillside. The proposer appeared to be motivated by the thought that artisans might act as rangers to prevent boys trespassing, rather than to provide labour on the course. The purchase of badges for artisans to wear in 1936 confirms that a section was formed and suggests that the duties included ranging. In 1937 the *Suggestion Book* included an entry that artisans should act as fore-caddies for the blind drive, over the hill, on the 16th hole. Southport and Ainsdale has had an artisan section only since 1937 and Hesketh's artisan section came into existence as late as 1938.

Artisan sections normally had a programme of competitions and inter-club matches with other local artisans. At Hillside a member gave a trophy for competition and the Club's support for artisan golf was demonstrated when it hosted the 12th North of England Artisan Golf Tournament in 1939. Playing in this tournament J. Shortall, a Hillside artisan and a painter by trade, won the *News of the World* Challenge Cup. Playing off the handicap limit of 18, he had a nett score of 150 for 36 holes.

Unlike the artisan sections of the other three major Southport clubs, that at Hillside did not survive the Second World War, but after the war finished the Board considered reviving it. In 1951 the Green Committee proposed the '...erection of an Artisans' shed in the caddies' enclosure' alongside the railway. No action was taken but in 1961 a revival of the section was proposed by Freddie Veale. After several meetings and consultation with S&A about their scheme, the Board decided in favour of again having an artisan section. The Green Committee agreed playing times and conditions and arrangements were put in place for a meeting with prospective members. The Board then decided that '...the present is not the most appropriate time to proceed' and the matter was shelved. In 1970, the Green Committee again put forward a proposal to establish an artisan section to the Board. This suggestion appeared to vanish from view. Ironically the Club did subsequently employ artisans from Royal Birkdale and S&A to undertake divoting duties.

The Clubhouse

The new clubhouse was opened in December 1924 (Fig.36). The two-storey, square, brick-built building, with a roof of an unusual pyramidal design, had a ground floor verandah and a first floor balcony, which was furnished with canvas backed chairs, overlooking the course. The larger surfaces of the outside walls were rendered in white stucco. Hastings Road had not then been built and access was via a cinder track from the Waterloo Road direction (Fig.37). A new railway station, Hillside Station on Waterloo Road Bridge, and a bus service on Waterloo Road, which was started in 1925, gave access to the course. The Club unsuccessfully sought a right of way for a footpath across Corporation land alongside the railway to link the clubhouse to the station.

A photograph pasted into the Club scrapbook purports to show the original clubhouse 'shed' at Hill Side Farm (Fig.38). It was dated 1912 but the photograph shows a golfer driving on the 1st tee of the new course. Hillside Station, which was only opened in 1926, can be seen in the background. This tee was alongside the railway and behind the building line of the new clubhouse. The shed overlooked the 1st tee and was used by the professional prior to accommodation being provided

Fig.36 *The clubhouse 1924. This building can still be identified as the core of the current clubhouse. Note the open verandah area.*

for him in a clubhouse extension. It seems that the shed had been the original clubroom and had belonged to Peter Lloyd who sold it to the Club in 1924.

Fig.37 *The clubhouse 1930. This aerial view shows the approach track from Waterloo Road.*

Fig.38 *(Below) Driving off the 1st tee c.1930. The tee was located alongside the railway behind the rear of the clubhouse. Hillside railway station can be seen in the background.*

Financial constraints dictated that only modest improvements were initially made to the 1924 clubhouse. A bar hatch was installed to allow drinks to be served outside and crazy paving paths laid in front of the building. Despite the continuing financial problems a plan for further improvements was drawn up and approved by the Planning Committee of the Town Council in 1930, but it was 1933 before most of them were implemented. Increasing the mortgage substantially financed the scheme and additional money was raised for a general refurbishment fund, for example the proceeds of efforts by the ladies to raise money for a new carpet, in their lounge, were donated. The space under the verandah was enclosed and a bay window added, thus doubling the size of the smoke room. Over the new bay Hillside's large distinctive clock was installed. Improvements were made to the locker room, and photographs show that by 1934 there was a single-storey, flat roofed extension in place, on the railway side of the building. It included a room for the ladies, a new locker room, and a shop and workshop for the professional, with an open shelter for the caddies, facing the railway (Fig.39). A new fireplace was installed in the smoke room. J.G. Wilkinson again carried out the work. Member Walter Wright, a builder who had submitted the lowest tender for the original building, but had subsequently withdrawn it, provided oak panel boards for this principal club room (Fig.40). Another member gave 24 Lloyd Loom chairs and six tables.

Such was the post-war austerity that in 1951 members of the greenkeeping staff were deployed during bad weather to replace worn floor boards in the locker room. Clubhouse improvements had to wait for a few more years before Alfred Campion, a prominent Southport

Fig.39 *Clubhouse extension 1930s. The aerial view shows the extent of the extension. The verandah had been enclosed and the space incorporated into the men's lounge. A roadway led from the car parking area to the newly laid out Hastings Road.*

Fig.40 *Men's lounge 1955. The fireplace has now been removed to provide a new entrance. This group included Freddie Veale, exteme left, and Bert Collinge, third from the left.*

chartered architect and club member, who made his professional expertise available to the Club without any fees, was asked to draw up two schemes for the clubhouse, one a complete renovation and the other for a partial scheme. The budget version was chosen. Attention was given to catering, and from 1955 the first-floor dining room was extended by absorbing the balcony, and building out to the line of the smoke room front wall. Picture windows replaced the two dormer windows and brought a new look to the front façade (Fig.41). The kitchen was redesigned and quarters for the steward and stewardess provided. A room big enough to take two billiard tables was added on the ground floor to the west side of the clubhouse.

By 1958, the Club was again considering clubhouse extensions. The landowner, Southport Corporation, had imposed requirements of course and clubhouse improvement on its other two golf club tenants, Royal Birkdale and Hesketh, when it bought the land in the 1930s. Because of the financial difficulties that Hillside was then facing similar requirements were not demanded. In 1960, however, Chairman Bert Collinge told the members that the Club was '...under an obligation to bring our facilities into keeping with the requirements of a championship golf course.' Entry to the clubhouse had formerly been through a door on a sidewall. A new entrance on the car park replaced this and it led into a roomy new hall. The scheme also included a mixed cocktail bar at the rear of the clubhouse, alongside the car park. It was a room without windows that had originally been a toilet. When one member argued that a new cocktail bar should overlook the course John Moody, the Captain, replied that it '...should be a room where members of both sexes could meet and drink away from prying eyes and in reasonable comfort.' The cost of this new bar was met by a gift from one member and it was opened in December 1961 (Fig.42). Further developments undertaken over the next few years included an extension to the men's lounge, which was doubled in length, with picture windows overlooking the course (Fig.43). The ground floor extension included additions to the men's locker room, which was '...believed to be the largest on Merseyside', a replacement washroom, and a trolley store. Work was also done on the ladies' accommodation. This included providing a 'moveable wall' as 'sound proof as possible' so that their lounge could serve as an extension to the dining room. This 'improvement' was not popular with the ladies, particularly when assurances about the restricted nature of its use were not honoured. Members' loans played a significant part in financing the final £20,000 cost of the developments and the Hillside tradition of members donating gifts for specific purposes was again evident. Chairs, glass panels, the cost of decorating and flooring were all examples. Principal benefactors included Cyril Hodkinson MBE who furnished the alcove in the main lounge, provided the bar screen, fitted the cocktail bar and supplied seats, and Freddie Veale, who provided leather covered chairs for the men's lounge. The ladies furnished their new lounge.

Fig.41 *Dining room 1960s. This first floor room with its view over the course, had survived little changed.*

Bert Collinge and his peers certainly had the high ambitions for Hillside. When Collinge was captain, journalist Ben Wright wrote of the '...dream of the men behind this once overshadowed club to stage an Open Championship.' After 50 years Hillside undoubtedly had a first-class golf course and clubhouse. The author of an R&A publication in 2000 noted how development in the 1960s had seen the Club '...rapidly graduate to rank proudly alongside all its illustrious Lancashire neighbours.' At the AGM in 1970 the directors presented a piece of inscribed plate to Collinge, who, it was said, had been the moving spirit behind the improvements to both clubhouse and course. Although some members disliked his management style, few would deny him the right to be regarded as 'Mr Hillside'.

Fig.42 *The mixed cocktail bar 1960s. Such provision was the common contemporary response to attempts to increase access for ladies.*

Fig.43 *Men's lounge 1960s. This principal clubroom had been doubled in size (see Fig.40). One of the Lloyd Loom chairs is still in use.*

Chapter Five
Professional Tournaments
1923 - 1967
with a contribution by Jack Nicklaus

Joint Ventures with the Corporation

The purchase by the Corporation of the Hillside, Birkdale and Hesketh links was partially motivated by concern to retain open spaces and provide playing facilities for both residents and visitors, but there was also a wish to host professional tournaments in the town in order to attract spectators and generate publicity. There were few professional tournaments in the 1920s and sponsorship was rare. The 1930s saw Southport emerge as a major venue for professional tournament golf, and much of the credit for this development must go to Thomas Edwin Wolstenholme, who had been appointed in the early 1920s as the resort's first publicity manager. He had already made a major impact in the town by helping to establish the Southport Flower Show. He was then influential in persuading the authority to set up a Golf Tournament Committee, which included two representatives from each of the four major local clubs. It was this body that was responsible for promoting Southport as a centre for professional golf tournaments.

In May 1930, a **£1,500 Southport Professional Golf Tournament** was held in the town with two-day qualifying at Hillside, Hesketh, and S&A followed by four final rounds at Birkdale. The Southport Corporation and the *Daily Dispatch* jointly sponsored the event. There were no exemptions from qualification and the field at Hillside included Abe Mitchell, Sam Ryder's personal professional, who was approaching 50-years-of-age (Fig.44). Small in stature, Mitchell was one of the first giants of the game to play on the Hillside links.

The scores at Hillside generally were higher than elsewhere in the two qualifying rounds. 'It is a tricky course and provided the competitors with a stiff test.' Most

Fig.44 *Abe Mitchell with Sam Ryder. Peter Alliss states as '...a known fact' that the figure of the golfer on the lid of the Ryder Cup was modelled on Mitchell.*

consistent of all the players was the ex-British champion, Abe Mitchell, who had two rounds of 73 and an aggregate of 146, headed the list of those who qualified.

He was one of the few professionals who continued to use hickory clubs after the introduction of metal shafts. Mitchell, who was described as 'lashing' his shots, was said to have driven the green on Hillside's 296 yard long 8th hole. Significantly 76 of the 100 qualifiers for the final rounds at Birkdale used the new metal shafts that had been legalised in the November of the previous year.

In a letter to the Southport Corporation a *Daily Dispatch* representative wrote that the organisation at Southport had '...exceeded anything seen in connection with any previous tournament in this country.' The bottom line, however, was that the newspaper company had to cover a loss of £1,000 and withdrew its support (Fig.45).

In the following year the Dunlop Rubber Company joined the Corporation as joint sponsors of the **Dunlop-Southport 1,500 Guineas Tournament**, and shared the cost estimated at £2,000. The prize money was claimed to be the largest total offered for a tournament of this kind in Europe. It was sufficient to attract a field of 300, which included all the top British professionals and a small number from the United States, the Argentine, and some European countries.

All four of Southport's leading clubs were, at different times, to be venues for the qualifying rounds of what became the annual Dunlop-Southport Tournament (Fig.46). In 1933, Hillside was a qualifying course and A.J. Lacey established a new course record of 69. The final four rounds were played at neighbouring S&A and the winner was Bill Davies, the Ryder Cup player from Wallasey, whilst the runner-up was Henry Cotton.

The qualifying rounds returned to Hillside in 1935. Henry Cotton played at Hillside in the second round, when Bill Davies was one of the two leaders with a 71 (Fig.47). Cotton attracted '...a large gallery, but on the whole gave a

Fig.45 *Southport Professional Golf Tournament 1930. The marquee was Woodhead's refreshment tent. Spectators are coming through the tented turnstile and the Club flag flies proudly from the mast.*

disappointing display, returning a 79.' Following the final rounds at Birkdale the first prize of £315 and a Dunlop gold wristlet watch was won by Ryder Cup captain Charles Whitcombe with Cotton in a share of second place.

Cotton was again amongst the competitors playing one of their qualifying rounds at Hillside when the event returned in 1937 (Fig.48). Despite hooking his opening drive onto the railway he carded a 72; whilst Charlie Whitcombe set a record of 66 for the recently altered course. Hillside professional John Burton's brother Dick won the tournament. A feature of the Dunlop-Southport tournaments in the late 1930s was the participation of Polly Wingate, Britain's only lady professional tournament golfer.

Henry Cotton dominated British professional golf in this era, and was able to break the stranglehold that American golfers had exerted on the Open Championship, eventually winning it four times. He took British professional golf to a new level, both on and off the course. Through his game, style of living, manner and attitude, he helped to elevate the previously depressed status of professional golfers in this country. There were only about eight national tournaments a year, and it was impossible for professionals to make a living from tournaments alone. They had to rely on their regular income as club professionals. Tournaments at this time finished with 36 holes on a Friday in order to allow the players to return to their shops and serve the members at the weekend. Cotton's stubborn independent streak was well illustrated by his refusal to enter the 1938 Dunlop-Southport Tournament. He described the event as a 'marathon', and particularly objected to the requirement for all the players to play two qualifying rounds, prior to the 72 holes competition, with the possibility of a play-off over a further 36 holes.

By the late 1930s the clubs which had previously supported the Dunlop-Southport Tournament appear to have lost some of their enthusiasm. In 1939 Birkdale refused to host it claiming that its course was overplayed. S&A decided that its course also needed a rest; whilst Hesketh's newly laid-out course had not settled down. As only Hillside was willing to participate the tournament was cancelled, a decision that was then overtaken by the outbreak of war.

After the war the Dunlop-Southport was re-started in 1946 (Fig.49). Henry Cotton was drawn to play at Hillside, his partner on the day withdrew and Hillside's Bert Collinge, who then had a handicap of seven, played with him as his marker. Press photographs show the stewards, dubbed 'Southport lancers', using long canes, topped with pennants, to form barriers to control the galleries. As the Corporation's share of overall cost of the tournament was £1,480 it decided to pull out and there was no competition in 1947. Following representations from the Dunlop Company, Southport agreed to be involved in 1948. Hillside was again a qualifying course and the home professional, John Burton, broke his own two-year-old record for the changed course by two strokes with a round of 67. After the 72 holes of the final there was a tie and a 36 holes play-off followed. The winner was Ulsterman Fred Daly, who also won the Open Championship in that year. Such were the escalating costs of this competition that the Corporation had to find £3,000 as its 50 per cent contribution. This proved to be too expensive and the Dunlop-Southport Tournament was dropped, with Hillside, unlike Southport's three other championship courses, never having been invited to host the final four rounds.

Southport and the Ryder Cup

In November 1932, the secretary of the Professional Golfers' Association wrote to the Southport Town Council announcing that its committee had decided to play the 1933 Ryder Cup at Southport on a course and on dates to be arranged later. It now seems impossible that the arrangements could be so vague a few months before the event. Later in a letter of thanks to the local authority, the PGA secretary identified T.E. Wolstenholme, the town's Publicity Manager who had forged strong links with the association, as the man responsible for bringing the event to Southport. It was he who persuaded the Council to invite the PGA to stage the match in Southport, but on which course would it be played? Following the purchase by the Corporation of the Birkdale and Hesketh courses they were being

Fig.48 *The Dunlop-Southport Tournament 1936. Henry Cotton putting on the 6th green at S&A. Beyond the railway on the right is Hawes House. The 8th tee of the Hillside course was to the left of the trees. Further left, players can be seen putting on the 9th green. The tall sand dunes on which the short 11th hole sat can be seen in the background.*

Fig.46 *(Top Left) The Dunlop-Southport Tournament – a season ticket 1931.*

Fig.47 *(Bottom Left) The Dunlop-Southport 1935. This Ryder Cup player, Bill Davies of Wallasey, was one of the top tournament professionals, but, golf shoes in hand, he had to carry his own equipment*

reconstructed to bring them up to championship standard. Birkdale would have been the preference of the local authority but J.H. Taylor, the Ryder Cup captain, was one of the course architects for the reconstruction at Birkdale, and he knew that it would not be ready in time. He also knew that James Braid's revision of the S&A course had been completed earlier. Hillside's 1923 course appears not have been considered and Wolstenholme advised the Council to nominate S&A. The attendance of the Prince of Wales vastly boosted the crowds and the event was such a success that it returned to S&A in 1937. There was speculation that Southport would become the permanent home venue for the Ryder Cup.

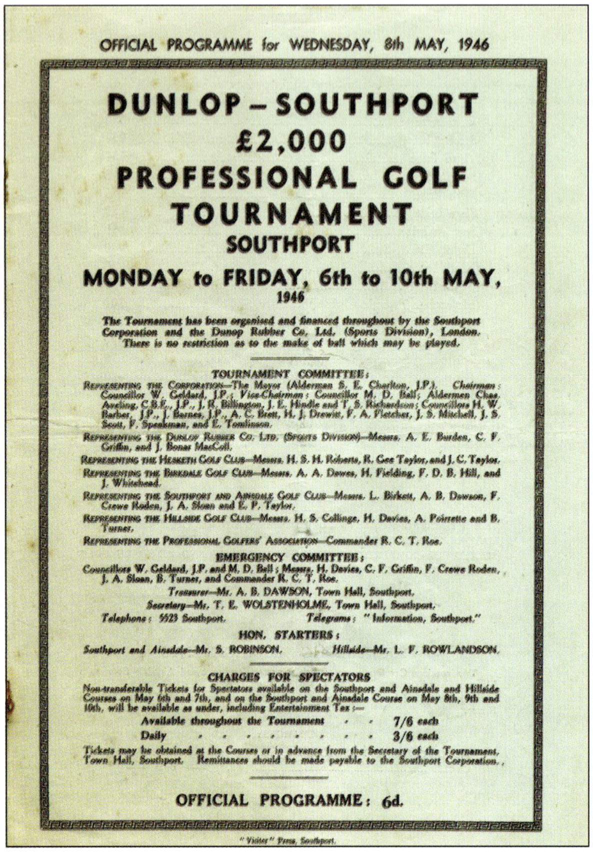

OFFICIAL PROGRAMME for WEDNESDAY, 8th MAY, 1946

DUNLOP – SOUTHPORT
£2,000
PROFESSIONAL GOLF
TOURNAMENT
SOUTHPORT

MONDAY to FRIDAY, 6th to 10th MAY,
1946

The Tournament has been organised and financed throughout by the Southport Corporation and the Dunop Rubber Co. Ltd. (Sports Division), London. There is no restriction as to the make of ball which may be played.

TOURNAMENT COMMITTEE:

REPRESENTING THE CORPORATION—The Mayor (Alderman S. E. Charlton, J.P.). *Chairman*: Councillor W. Geldard, J.P.; *Vice-Chairman*: Councillor M. D. Ball; Aldermen Chas. Aveling, C.B.E., J.P., J. R. Billington, J. E. Hindle and T. S. Richardson; Councillors H. W. Barber, J.P., J. Barnes, J.P., A. C. Brett, H. J. Drewitt, F. A. Fletcher, J. S. Mitchell, J. S. Scott, F. Speakman, and E. Tomlinson.

REPRESENTING THE DUNLOP RUBBER CO. LTD. (SPORTS DIVISION)—Messrs. A. E. Burden, C. F. Griffin, and J. Bonar MacColl.

REPRESENTING THE HESKETH GOLF CLUB—Messrs. H. S. H. Roberts, R. Gee Taylor, and J. C. Taylor.

REPRESENTING THE BIRKDALE GOLF CLUB—Messrs. A. A. Dewes, H. Fielding, F. D. B. Hill, and J. Whitehead.

REPRESENTING THE SOUTHPORT AND AINSDALE GOLF CLUB—Messrs. L. Birkett, A. B. Dawson, F. Crewe Roden, J. A. Sloan and E. P. Taylor.

REPRESENTING THE HILLSIDE GOLF CLUB—Messrs. H. S. Collinge, H. Davies, A. Poirrette and B. Turner.

REPRESENTING THE PROFESSIONAL GOLFERS' ASSOCIATION—Commander R. C. T. Roe.

EMERGENCY COMMITTEE:

Councillors W. Geldard, J.P. and M. D. Bell; Messrs. H. Davies, C. F. Griffin, F. Crewe Roden, J. A. Sloan, B. Turner, and Commander R. C. T. Roe.

Treasurer—Mr. A. B. DAWSON, Town Hall, Southport.
Secretary—Mr. T. E. WOLSTENHOLME, Town Hall, Southport.
Telephone: 5523 Southport. *Telegrams*: "Information, Southport."

HON. STARTERS:

Southport and Ainsdale—Mr. S. ROBINSON. *Hillside*—Mr. L. F. ROWLANDSON.

CHARGES FOR SPECTATORS

Non-transferable Tickets for Spectators available on the Southport and Ainsdale and Hillside Courses on May 6th and 7th, and on the Southport and Ainsdale Course on May 8th, 9th and 10th, will be available as under, including Entertainment Tax:—

Available throughout the Tournament . . . 7/6 each
Daily . . . . 3/6 each

Tickets may be obtained at the Courses or in advance from the Secretary of the Tournament, Town Hall, Southport. Remittances should be made payable to the Southport Corporation.

OFFICIAL PROGRAMME: 6d.

"Visiter" Press, Southport.

Fig.49 *Dunlop-Southport Tournament 1946. The list of corporation and club officials on this programme cover reveals the way in which professional golf tournaments in Southport were organised during this period.*

The Open Championship Qualifying

The Open Championship was scheduled to be played for the first time at Birkdale in 1941, but the war prevented this from happening and it was **1954** before the R&A awarded the championship to the now Royal Birkdale. At this time, the entire field had to qualify over two rounds (Monday and Tuesday) on the Championship course and a neighbouring course. Hillside was the designated qualifying course and the entry included the legendary American 57-year-old Gene Sarazen. He was a two-time winner of the American Open, three-time winner of the American PGA Championship, a former winner of the Open Championship and a player in six successive Ryder Cup matches. He was a gracious competitor and, at Hillside, he charmed the gallery whilst returning a 67. Another notable competitor at Hillside was, four-time Open Champion, South African Bobby Locke (Fig.50). For the Champion, Australian Peter Thomson, it was the first of his five Open titles; it was also the first of three consecutive victories. Between 1952 and 1958, this supreme exponent of links golf never finished worse than second. The Championship was to provide the winner, twenty-four-year-old Australian Peter Thomson, who was playing regularly on the American tour, with prize money of £750. Thomson, a precise ball striker, had a great command of flight and had the vision required to play links golf well. His judgement of where to pitch the ball to enable it to run out to the hole was outstanding. His relaxed approach was perhaps exemplified by the casual manner in which he tapped in the final short putt using the back of his putter. His cavalier approach was demonstrated by his choice of clubs, he apparently played with a new set, which he had borrowed from one of the manufacturers immediately prior to the tournament. For over a decade Locke and Thomson dominated this championship. Former Hillside member, amateur Jackie Wroe, qualified for all four rounds at Royal Birkdale.

1954 was the last of the three-day Open Championships, with two rounds being played on the final day, a Friday. In the following year the BBC televised the Open for the first time and paid the R&A a fee of £150 for the rights to broadcast both the Open and the Walker Cup match.

When the Open returned to Royal Birkdale in **1961** final qualifying was still restricted to two courses: Royal Birkdale and Hillside. During the qualifying competition Ryder Cup captain Dai Rees set a new course record of 66 at Hillside and Tony Coop, a local boy and former Hillside junior member, who was the professional at Dean Wood, came near to sharing it with a 67 (Fig.51). Rees went on to finish as runner-up, at Royal Birkdale, a single shot behind the Champion Arnold Palmer. The completion of the championship was threatened by appalling weather and Palmer, whose presence did so much to revive the flagging fortunes of the

Fig.50 *Open Championship Qualifying 1954. Four times Open Champion Bobby Locke leaving the 16th (now the 9th) green. He is wearing his trade mark white flat cap and white shoes but unusually he was not wearing plus fours. This area of the course was flat and featureless at this time.*

Fig.51 *Open Championship Qualifying 1961. Ryder Cup captain Dai Rees playing out of a bunker. In those days of austerity and formality, the gallery wore street clothing.*

Fig.52 *The Open Championship at Royal Birkdale 1965. Five times Open Champion Peter Thomson with his regular caddie, Bobby (Jackie) Leigh. Leigh was one of the famous four 'Birkdale Caddies', who were close neighbours in Suffolk Road and caddied for seven Open Champions. Leigh's mother worked behind the bar at Hillside.*

Open, played what Peter Alliss described as '...some of the greatest golf ever seen in gale-force winds.' Palmer had played in a qualifying round at Hillside.

In 1963 the R&A introduced exemptions for 44 players with qualification for the other 76. The Open returned to Royal Birkdale in **1965** and Hillside was one of the two chosen qualifying courses. The exempted golfers could play practice rounds on the championship course on the Monday and Tuesday, with the public having to pay an admission charge. There was no charge for the qualifying rounds and spectators had the opportunity to walk round the course with leading professionals and watch them build their round. Jimmy Hitchcock carded a 67 at Hillside, one outside the course record. The Champion was again Australian Peter Thomson (Fig.52).

It was not, however, golfing stars who made the headlines in the qualifying rounds at Hillside in 1965. The R&A was to realise just how 'Open' the Championship was. One of the competitors was Walter Danecki and the appearance and demeanour of this 43-year-old did nothing to suggest that he was not the professional golfer he had claimed to be on his entry form. On the 1st tee his swing immediately raised doubts, which were confirmed by his score of 112. Questioned by R&A officials, he revealed that he was a postman from Milwaukee. 'It was visions of getting my hands on that crock of gold that made me do it. I wanted to see my name on the cup alongside Arnold Palmer.' Official assumptions that, chastened by his experience, he would quietly disappear were not to be fulfilled. The following day he was again on the tee waiting for his starting time. Two balls over the railway on the 1st hole followed by an eight on the 2nd heralded a score of 116. He was to miss qualifying for the final rounds by 88 shots. But undaunted by his experience, he told waiting reporters that: 'I want to say that your English ball is perfect for these conditions. If I had been using the big ball, I'd have been in all sorts of trouble.'

Other Professional Competitions

Outside the joint ventures with the Corporation, and the meetings of the Liverpool Alliance there were no professional tournaments played at Hillside in the pre-war period.

After the demise of the Dunlop-Southport tournament in 1948 a variety of competitions was hosted. In 1955 qualifying rounds for the **Swallow-Penfold Tournament** at S&A were played at Hillside. The participation of the home professional John Burton attracted particular interest in the **Martini Northern Professional Golfers' Foursomes**, in 1959. Sadly he and his partner lost their opportunity to win with a disastrous seven on the 18th hole. The winning cheque (£75) emphasised the modest nature of remuneration in regional events. The **Liverpool and District Open Championship** was played at Hillside in 1957 and was won by Tony Coop. The **Liverpool and District Assistants' Championship** was hosted in 1959, when Dennis Scanlon, who had been an assistant to John Burton for five years, won the event. He left Hillside to join Henry Cotton as an assistant. 1964 saw the **Northern Professional Championship** played at Hillside; Hedley Muscroft was the champion after a tie with Tony Coop. Coop enjoyed a relatively successful tournament career and was a winner of several long driving competitions, which featured in tournaments at that time.

1962 saw the advent of a new era in professional golf at Hillside. There was an opportunity to see 22-year-old Jack Nicklaus, the rising star of American golf, playing at Hillside

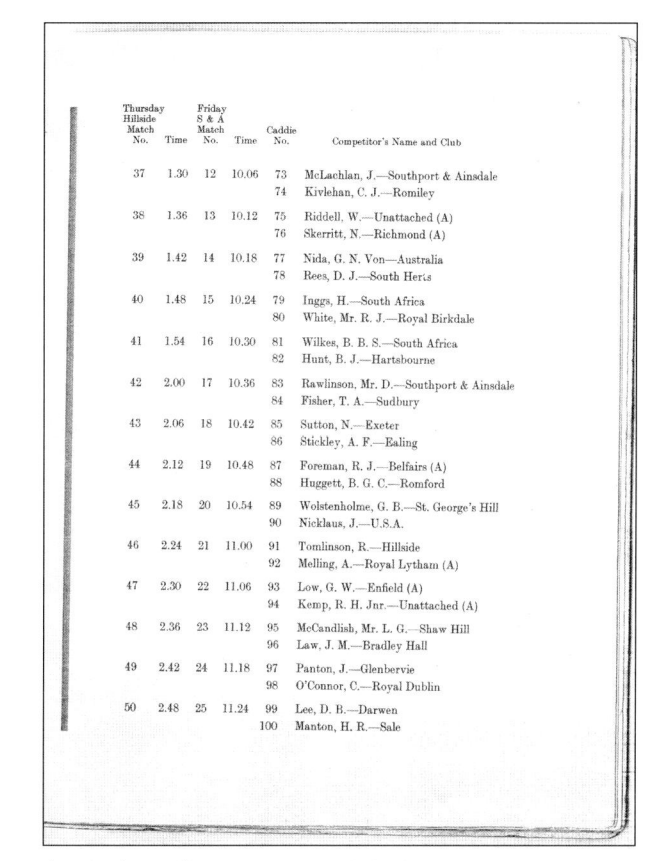

Fig.53 *Piccadilly Tournament 1962. The draw.*

Fig.54 *Piccadilly Tournament 1962. Jack Nicklaus wearing Edith Swift's hat. The second golfer is Dai Rees.*

in what was his first professional tournament in this country. The Club was hosting this international event on behalf of Carreras, the tobacco company who were promoting a new brand of cigarettes – Piccadilly. Every competitor played one of his two qualifying rounds at S&A and one at Hillside, whilst the two final rounds were at Hillside. It was the first professional tournament in England to finish on a Sunday. Jack Nicklaus, who had a glittering amateur record, later described his participation in this **Piccadilly Tournament** as one of the dumbest things of his professional career. In his autobiography he wrote that in these early days as a professional: 'I was still not absolutely sure of my earning capabilities as a pro' and '…decided that this might be an opportunity for some easy pickings.' The total prize money was £8,000, with £2,000 for the winner. These were the highest figures that had been played for in Great Britain, and the highest ever outside America (Fig.53).

In July 2010, Jack Nicklaus kindly wrote to the Club setting out his thoughts on Hillside Golf Club:

> When asked about success, whether on the golf course or off, be it in business or in life, I have always said that being prepared is chief among the reasons behind achieving success. In fact, my wife Barbara always said, 'There is no excuse for not being properly prepared.' I guess I had no excuse in May of 1962 and certainly no one but myself to blame for my first professional showing across the pond.
>
> Hillside Golf Club is where I played my first pro round on a seaside links course. Hillside is a dramatic layout in Southport, England, situated immediately adjacent to Royal Birkdale, and alongside Southport and Ainsdale. In May of 1962 – my first season as a professional – they held the inaugural Piccadilly Tournament, arguably the first significant event hosted by a club already steeped in history and tradition. I had accepted an invitation to play in the Piccadilly, and flew directly from the Colonial in Texas, arriving just two days ahead of the tournament. What awaited me was an event both forgettable and unforgettable. Forgettable in that I played poorly, finishing 43rd after rounds of 79-71-70-78. Unforgettable in the lessons I learned.
>
> When I left Fort Worth Texas, the temperatures were in the 90s. When I arrived at Hillside on the northwest coast of England, it was cold, wet and windy. I later started to refer to it as three-sweater weather. But I didn't arrive with three sweaters or anything close. In fact when I couldn't purchase the suitable attire to handle the elements, I believe that it was a female member of Hillside who loaned me a hand-knitted woolly hat that I gladly donned on the first tee (Fig.54).
>
> In addition to the weather, the time difference caught up with me, as did the smaller British golf ball we played at the time (Fig.55). The confluence of those necessary adjustments - or lack thereof - led to a difficult flight home, and soul searching thoughts of why I believed I could simply jump across the Atlantic, show up in very different conditions and expect success. That first visit to Hillside taught me that if I was going to go play seaside golf in the U.K., then I better bring along a different game than I brought along that week.
>
> A month after my visit to Hillside, I was fortunate to win the US Open - my first professional victory and first major championship. But more important was the lesson learned about seaside links and being prepared, a lesson I applied to my next four decades of seaside links and Open Championship golf. Today that lesson learned at Hillside is a significant reason why I enjoyed success over those decades, and why I have such an affinity and respect for the challenges of true links golf.

Fig.55 *Piccadilly Tournament 1962. Nicklaus with his caddy – Bill Tomlinson - and an unfamiliar set of irons which he was contracted to use. Bill's five sons were all professional golfers. One of them, Reg, was an assistant at Hillside and played in the pair behind Nicklaus in the first two rounds of this tournament (See Fig.53).*

Of his performance at Hillside, the *Southport Visiter* noted that the '...most disappointing feature of a day of fine golf was the failure of the American golfer, Jack Nicklaus, to live up to his high reputation.' After his first round of 79, Barrie Ward, a golf journalist, described him being '...slumped on a bench in the Hillside locker room with tears as big as peas rolling down his broad face.' Peter Thomson won the event, and the quality of the field was demonstrated by the fact that the next five places were filled by Christy O'Connor, Max Faulkner (The 1951 Open Champion who equalled the Hillside course record with a 66), Bernard Hunt, Dai Rees and Harry Weetman. Jack Nicklaus later claimed that one positive outcome from this 1962 visit to Hillside was that his playing partner, Guy Wolstenholme, a former Walker Cup player and father of Gary, introduced him to the game of snooker.

Notwithstanding Nicklaus's travails, the success of the Piccadilly confirmed Hillside as a top-class tournament venue. With its developing course, Hillside was emerging from the shadow of its illustrious neighbours.

Chapter Six
Club Matters at Hillside
1923 - 1967

The Club Professionals

Jerry Bond 1923-1927

Thirty-year-old Jerry Bond replaced his brother Fred as professional in 1923, having previously been employed as one of David McEwan's assistants at Birkdale Golf Club. He lived in one of the satellite cottages of Balshaw's Farm, which, prior to the building of Waterloo New Road, was a near neighbour of Peter Lloyd's Hill Side Farm, and it is highly likely that, like his brother Fred, he gained his introduction to golf as a boy caddie. As an assistant at Birkdale, he established a reputation as both a club maker and a teacher.

McEwan had allowed Jerry limited opportunities to play in tournaments. He survived the qualifying and first round of the 1921 *News of the World* Tournament, and in 1922 he tied for second place in the qualifying round for the North of England Professional Tournament. In 1923 he was third in the Liverpool and District Championship.

After his move to Hillside, Bond continued to play in competitions at this regional level and furthered the Club's link with the Liverpool and District Golf Alliance. He regularly represented the Alliance in the annual fixture with the Manchester Alliance and in 1925 he won the Liverpool and District Open Championship, the first open event won by a player from Hillside. Playing at the national level he qualified for the Open Championship at Hoylake in 1924 with a score of 151, one shot better than American Ryder Cup captain Walter Hagen. The ten players in front of him included James Braid and J.H. Taylor, two of the 'Great Triumvirate' of champions. In the following year he defeated the 54-year-old J.H. Taylor in the first round of the *News of the World* Tournament, but was then beaten in the third (Fig.56).

Bond was a popular teacher, but members of other golf clubs who came to him for a lesson had to pay a green fee to the financially challenged Club in addition to his charge. Despite Hillside's financial problems, Bond was granted a modest salary increase but in October 1927 he was released from his contract in order to allow him to take up an appointment with West Lancashire Ladies' Golf Club, which was at this time a prosperous independent club run by the ladies, with its own course, clubhouse and professional.

Fig.56 *Jerry Bond. A. Moscrop, whose sporting cartoons appeared regularly in the Liverpool Echo, was the grandfather of Pam Green, the Lady Captain in 2006.*

Laurie Cawkwell 1928-1930

Jerry Bond was replaced at Hillside by Laurie Cawkwell, an assistant to his uncle, the professional at the West Lancashire Golf Club. He had previously been an apprentice professional at Skegness. Cawkwell had an unusual educational background for a professional golfer having attended a selective secondary school in Leicester until he was 16. Would-be professionals generally progressed from elementary school to caddying and then to becoming an apprentice professional. The *Southport Visiter* described him as '…one of the new school of young golf professionals.' At Skegness he had had considerable experience as a teacher and had developed skills as a clubmaker. Whilst with his uncle at West Lancashire he had been responsible for all the clubmaking and repairs in the shop, but had been given the opportunity to play in some local tournaments.

Cawkwell had limited success in Liverpool and District Alliance meetings; he won one meeting and was the runner-up in another, whilst playing with Bert Collinge and played for the Alliance against the Manchester Alliance. He set a course record of 67 at Hillside, but in 1930 he resigned and abandoned golf as a profession.

John Burton (1930-1972)

John Burton replaced Cawkwell after serving for five years as the professional at Darwen Golf Club. He was one of three brothers from a weaving family whose boyhood home overlooked the Darwen course and their introduction to the game was hitting bobbins with home-made clubs. Later each of them served a stint as Darwen's professional. Whilst there, John had enjoyed success in the Manchester and District Golf Alliance, winning its championship, and was runner-up in the Northern Championship.

At Hillside his retainer was £2 per week, plus an additional 15sh (75p) for taking charge of the course. He was allowed the opportunities to parade his golfing talents regularly on the national stage. In 1932 he qualified for the match play stages of the £1,000 *News of the World* Tournament at Moor Park, but made little further progress. He did better at Royal Porthcawl in 1933 in the Penfold-Porthcawl £750 Tournament. Several members of the American and British Ryder Cup teams were in the quality field, including past and future winners of the Open Championship. Burton followed a first round 71 with a course record of 67 for a seven shot lead. Despite closing rounds of 79 and 75, his score of 292 was sufficient for him to win the event and Hillside presented him with an additional ten guineas (£10.50p) to mark the occasion. This success gained him selection for an England team against Ireland.

Fig.57 *Dunlop-Southport Tournament 1948. John Burton driving. He was wearing the popular zipped waterproof jacket.*

Burton was to win the Liverpool and District Open Championship in 1939 and after the war he was to repeat this success on five further occasions. He was a committed participant in alliance golf, so much so that he frequently played in a Fylde Alliance tournament in the morning and then dashed by car to play in a Liverpool Alliance fixture in the afternoon. One reporter suggested that if he was not in the first three in both, his game was very much below form. He was a regular competitor in the annual Dunlop-Southport tournaments, but strangely he did not have a good record in the final rounds of this event (Fig.57).

In 1946 he finished as runner-up to Australian professional Norman Von Nida in the *News Chronicle* £1,500 Tournament at Brighton. Two years later he broke his own course record at Hillside by two strokes with a 67, and in the following year he and his partner Max Faulkner, (a future Open Champion) won the Professional Foursomes Tournament at South Herts. The final was decided by '…a particularly wicked stymie on the 17th green.' (Before the days of marking and lifting balls on the green, a stymie occurred when a ball blocked the route of one's opponent's ball to the hole. The victim had to play round or over the obstruction, and a penalty was incurred if the ball was touched.) The only option open to his opponent, brother Dick Burton, was to attempt to lob the ball over the blocking ball and into the tin. His attempt failed. A rule change, in 1952, took the stymie out of the game.

Burton's mid-career vein of rich form continued and, in 1947, he was the holder of five trophies. Burton was reported to hate the Old Course at St Andrew's. Apparently whilst staying there in 1939, the year in which his brother Dick won the Open Championship, he was heard to say, '…loudly in his characteristic forthright Lancashire manner,' that: 'If I had my way I would roll it up and take it out into the Atlantic and dump it.' Ten years later, however, the 46-year-old was again in St Andrew's and after four rounds of the Dunlop Master's tournament, he was tied for the £300 first prize with Charlie Ward, the diminutive Ryder Cup player. He lost the 36 holes play-off for what would probably have been his premier tournament achievement.

Opportunities for seniors were few but as he moved into his 50s, in addition to his local successes, he won the Northern Professional Championship at Seaton Carew and when the Teachers' Senior Tournament was added to the tournament calendar in 1957, he won the inaugural event at Fulwell. This win meant that Burton represented Great Britain in an International Seniors' Trophy match against the American Ryder Cup veteran Al Watrous, a game he lost.

A big man, it was argued that John Burton's style had not got the effortless fluency of his brother Dick. An article in *Golfing* noted that the 53-year-old was '…one of the strongest of professionals' and was one of the few first-class players who regularly used a number one iron. Another commentator attributed his long hitting with iron clubs to his powerful hands. Peter Alliss described him as '…one of the finest long-iron players I had ever seen' adding that he was known in the trade as 'Cleeky John!'

Despite his commitment to playing tournament golf, he had what some deemed to be unusual ideas about preparation. It seems that he rarely played a course in practice and when playing locally in tournaments, he also usually managed to find time to give lessons at Hillside. One reporter wrote that: 'His most earnest friends believe that if he approached the professional tournaments in the accepted way he would always finish in the top flight.' Perhaps his ways were merely those of an old fashioned professional.

When the Open Championship was played at Royal Birkdale in 1965, 61-year-old John posted a qualifying score but then withdrew from the championship proper. He told reporters that he '…did not fancy playing for four rounds on Royal Birkdale at my age.' Those who knew him thought that he enjoyed the satisfaction of having qualified and was happy to release his place for a younger professional.

In 1951, after 21 years' service at Hillside, Burton was elected an Honorary Life Member. In 1960 he was presented with a gold watch and to mark his retirement in 1972 he received a pair of binoculars. It was said that during his 42 years of service at Hillside, this presentation was only the second occasion on which John had been in the main lounge. In thanking the Club, John said that: 'The changes made over the years had brought the Club on a par with the greatest.' He had enjoyed extraordinarily good health during his time at Hillside and was proud of never having missed a day through sickness. Sadly, after an all too brief retirement, he died in 1973.

As with many contemporary club professionals there are numerous stories concerning his parsimony as a salesman, there are also those who tell of his generosity, when he thought it to be appropriate. When he retired he made a handsome donation towards the provision of the clubroom, alongside the spike bar, for junior members.

John Burton was a much-liked and well-respected member of his profession. His values were traditional golf values, and he was meticulous in observing conventions. When sports' shirts had become almost universal wear for golfers, he remained a collar and tie man. In his lifetime he had seen and experienced extraordinary changes in the status of professional golfers. Nevertheless, although a car owner, he continued to cycle to the Club not wanting the members to think that he was either pretentious, or affluent. Irlam's description of him being 'the golf professionals' professional' appears to fit the man.

His humanity was discreetly revealed in his sensitive encouragement of young professionals. He was a natural leader and in addition to his long stint as Captain of the Liverpool Alliance, he was a member of the executive of the PGA, and the secretary of its Northern Section. Members of the Northern PGA still play annually for the John Burton Trophy.

Domestic Club Competitions

We know nothing of any major club competition that might have been played on the Hill Side Farm course prior to 1923. As with so many of the aspects of the Hillside Club, it was from this date that there was a surge of activity. The opening of the temporary 18-hole course, in 1923, was celebrated by a mixed foursomes competition. The winning pair included Miss E.A. Lawrenson, who had been the first winner of the Lady Captain's Prize in the previous year. In 1923 the **President's Cup**, presented by R.F. Castleman was the first men's competition to be played on the temporary course, and N. Corkill won this 18 holes medal. It appears likely that there was not room for a president and a powerful chairman of the Board and Hillside soon became a club without a president or a president's trophy. Hillside's oldest surviving men's competition is the **Captain's Prize** and the first recorded winner, in 1923, was R. Bolton, over 36 holes, again played on the temporary hybrid course.

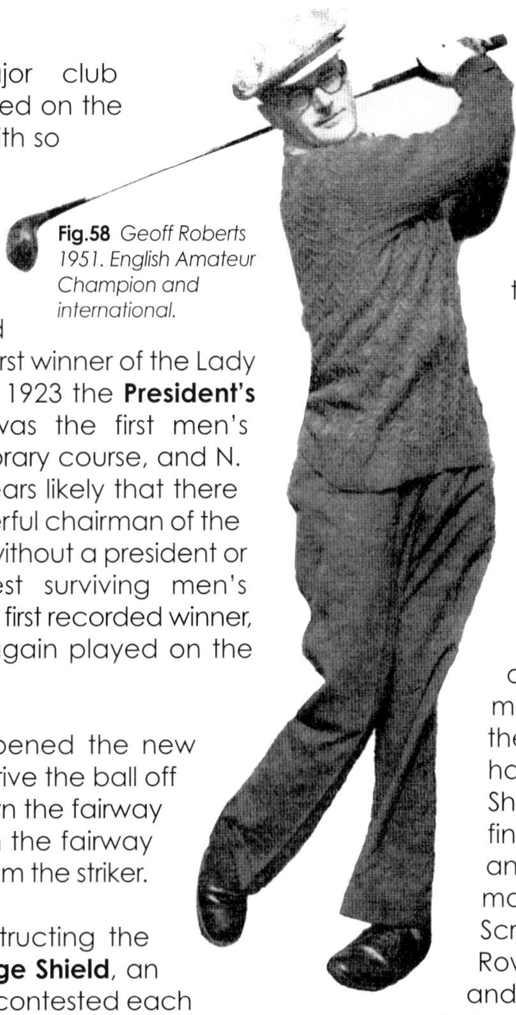

The Mayor of Southport officially opened the new course in 1924, when he attempted to drive the ball off the 1st tee, with the caddies waiting down the fairway to retrieve it. A large divot sailed down the fairway whilst the ball came to rest a few yards from the striker.

The contractor responsible for constructing the course, presented the **Conway Challenge Shield**, an 18 holes medal competition, which was contested each year until 1933, when it disappeared from the calendar. The **YMCA Trophy**, that marked the early links between the two clubs, is another lapsed competition. Mark Malies presented the Malies Prize in 1924, and the first winner was George Keeley. This competition became the **Malies Cup**, an 18 holes handicap competition. 1931 saw the introduction of the **Aggregate Trophy**. Club Chairman, Louis Rowlandson, presented the **Rowlandson Trophy**, for an 18 holes medal competition, in 1933. In the same year a general practitioner, Doctor William Lonen, presented the **Lonen Trophy**, an 18 holes medal competition for golfers with a handicap greater than 18. Not surprisingly this rapidly acquired the nickname of the 'Rabbits' Cup'. **The Founders' Trophy**, a 36 holes handicap event, was added to the honours' board in 1934.

The post-war years saw the introduction of further trophies predominantly for the more accomplished golfers. Captain Cyril Hodkinson, a generous benefactor of the Club, presented the **Scratch Trophy** in 1947. 1953 saw the **Ex-Captain's Four Ball** competition being added to the calendar. From the following year the **Hugh Davies Trophy**, for a 36 holes competition, was played in memory of this long-serving secretary. Having qualified for the final stages of the *Daily Mirror* North of England Tournament, scratch team player Mike Buckels won a '...thrilling final' at S&A. In addition to his personal prize an award to the Club was used to initiate the **Mike Buckels Match Play Trophy** in 1967. Mike was to become the second winner of this trophy in 1968.

Fig.58 Geoff Roberts 1951. English Amateur Champion and international.

A study of the 'gold paint' on the Club's honours' boards reveals the outstanding competition records of several members. Edward Darrah, a junior player on the old nine-hole course, reduced his handicap to one and won the first Conway Shield competition and was twice the beaten finalist in the Captain's Prize. Between 1948 and 1954, Charlie Blackshaw (Junior) won 13 major competitions at Hillside. He won the Scratch Trophy six times, the Aggregate and Rowlandson twice, and the Founders' Prize and the Hugh Davies Trophy once each. Between 1947 and 1949 Jackie Wroe won the Scratch Trophy on two occasions, along with the Malies Cup and Aggregate Trophy. Geoff Roberts, the son of S&A's professional and that club's distinguished amateur international and English Amateur Champion, was also a member of Hillside and won the Scratch Trophy four times and the Captain's Prize and the Ex-Captain's Four Ball competition twice each during the late 1950s (Fig.58). His regular participation in competitive golf at Hillside was not confined to the scratch trophies.

After Rowlandson, who was an indifferent golfer, the succession of Club chairmen demonstrated considerable golfing skills. Arnold Poirrette, playing to a handicap of between ten and 15, won the Malies Cup in 1931 and the Rowlandson Trophy in 1938. His successor, Bert Collinge, had a handicap as low as two, and Irlam notes that he was considered to be '…the best iron player in the Club.' Between 1930 and 1953, he won the Captain's Prize on three occasions, as well as winning the Malies Cup, the Aggregate Trophy and the YMCA Cup (Fig.59). Freddie Veale, who followed Bert Collinge as chairman, was also a single figure golfer. He was a former member of Childwall Golf Club, where he had won the Captain's Prize in 1939. Travelling to play at Hillside from his south Liverpool home, he won the Malies Cup twice as well as the Rowlandson Trophy and the Ex-Captain's Four Ball.

For 24 years secretary Hugh Davies closely supervised the men's Saturday competitions at Hillside. Playing partners were not chosen by the individual competitors or by a draw, but were 'selected' by Davies. He sat at a table in the lounge, collected the entry fees, gave out the scorecards and allocated the partners. He aimed to pair players who did not regularly play together in the belief that this would encourage the development of club morale. It was, however, a policy that caused much controversy.

Liverpool and District Golf Alliance

Professional Jerry Bond was an enthusiastic supporter of the Alliance and invited members to join him to play in its meetings. In December 1923 Bond and his partner, C. Thorley a 20-handicap golfer, playing in a 36 holes competition at Bromborough achieved Hillside's first known success in an outside meeting. In January 1925 the Alliance held the first of its many meetings at Hillside (Fig.60).

Fig.59 Captain's Prize 1932. Bert Collinge receiving the trophy from Captain Arnold Poirrette.

Laurie Cawkwell, Bond's short-lived successor as professional won an Alliance meeting at Hesketh with D.C. Andrews, who also took the prize for the best amateur score. In 1929, Walter Wright a 67-year-old five-handicap golfer won a 36 holes Alliance tournament at Hillside.

John Burton, who replaced Cawkwell in 1930, had an even stronger commitment to the Alliance than his predecessors and encouraged members to take part in its competitions. In 1930, Bert Collinge, with his partner Jerry Bond, Hillside's former professional, won an Alliance meeting at Hillside. Burton regularly invited the current Club captain to be his partner. A number of Hillside members won events partnering John Burton, whilst others played with professionals from other courses. Tom Johnson, the 1969 captain, won with the Haydock Park Club professional in 1960. Walter Wright was still participating in Alliance events in his 70s, frequently partnering John Burton. Pairings of two amateurs also played in the Alliance meetings. Harold James and Brian Shaw, two Hillside colts, won an am-am prize at Hillside in 1956. In one Alliance meeting in 1949, Hillside professional staff and members made a clean sweep and won all the prizes. The links between Hillside and the Alliance were strong; in the late 1950s Hillside Chairman Freddie Veale was the president of the Alliance, John Burton was the captain and Fred Hall, the Club secretary, was on the executive. Its H.S. Collinge Trophy marks Bert Collinge's contribution to the Alliance.

The Alliance ran the Spalding Cup, which had been presented by the Spalding Sports Company in about 1923, and was a popular competition with Hillside members. Open to amateurs and professionals, all competitors played off scratch in this foursomes' competition. After a qualifying competition, the leading four couples played match play.

Fig.60 *Liverpool Alliance c.1938. Driving from the 17th now the 10th tee. The corner of the clubhouse can be seen in the background.*

Fig.61 *John Burton and Charlie Blackshaw receiving the Spalding Cup. The player rear right was Ted Jarman, the 1935 Ryder Cup player.*

Cawkwell had several unsuccessful attempts to qualify, playing with Macauley and Darrah. Initially Burton played with Hillside's strongest player, one-handicap Edward Darrah, but they struggled to qualify for the match play stages and when they eventually surmounted this hurdle, in 1934, they lost in the semi-final. It was 1947 before Burton was to eventually win the cup when he and Charlie Blackshaw (Junior) were successful at Hillside. This pair repeated their success in 1949, again at Hillside, in 1955 and finally in 1964 (Fig.61). They were defeated finalists on two other occasions. Pairs of Hillside members regularly entered this event whilst some played with professionals from other clubs. Harold James got as far as the semi-final in 1964, when playing with Tony Coop.

The Lancashire Union of Golf Clubs

Hillside successfully applied to join the Lancashire Union of Golf Clubs in December 1922. The Union, founded in 1910, organises the annual county championship and runs the county team. Hillside did not have the depth of talent to produce a strong scratch team. Some of the Club's top players were attracted to join S&A, because it allowed them to play with probably the strongest group of players in club golf and thus enhance their chances of being selected for representative teams. Edward Darrah pioneered this route and played six games for Lancashire as an S&A member between 1936 and 1938, although he retained his Hillside membership up until his death in 1953. Jackie Wroe also gained county honours after joining S&A and went on to play 43 games over a 20-year period from 1950 and was the county champion in 1951. Charlie Blackshaw (Junior) was the first county player to be acknowledged in the Lancashire records as a Hillside member. Between 1951 and 1958, he won five and lost two of his seven county games. In 1957, Blackshaw also joined S&A.

It was 1935 before Hillside was invited to host a county match, when Lancashire beat Yorkshire by the narrowest of margins. The county returned to Hillside in 1953, when Lancashire comfortably defeated Staffordshire. The fixture had an added attraction for members of Hillside as Charlie Blackshaw and Jackie Wroe were both in the Lancashire team. The Club hosted the Lancashire Championship for the first time in 1954. It was memorable for Dixie Rawlinson of S&A whose morning qualifying score of 68, took three strokes off the amateur course record, which he followed up with a 70 in the afternoon to set a record qualifying score of 138. More significantly for Hillside, the Club team, anchored by Charlie Blackshaw, was to finish as runner-up to the all-conquering Southport and Ainsdale team. This was Hillside's first success in the Lancashire Team Championship. The Championship returned to Hillside in 1963. Bill Dickinson qualified for the match play stages and got through the first round. The champion was S&A's Geoff Roberts. Hillside hosted further county games, against Durham in 1964, and Yorkshire in 1966.

Liverpool Society of Golf Captains

Hillside applied to join the Liverpool Society of Golf Captains in 1934. The Society, which was founded in 1908, now includes members from 27 Merseyside and district clubs. In addition to an annual dinner, it organises several golfing events during each year (Fig.62). An individual prize for the best nett score, the Hayco Trophy, forms part of the Annual Competition. The first Hillside winner was Bert Collinge in 1938; Ben Turner won in 1948 and again in 1958. Arnold Poirrette won the trophy in 1952. Freddie Veale followed Ben's second success with a win in the following year. Since 1948, the Leverhulme Salver has been awarded to the club returning the best aggregate of three cards. Ben Turner, Bert Collinge and Arnold Poirrette won the trophy in its inaugural year. Further successes came in 1958 and 1961. As Bert Collinge was the Captain of the Society in that year, the Annual Meeting was held at Hillside for the first time.

Club Matches

There was little scratch team golf played during this period and prior to the 1950s the Hillside team made little impact in the team County Championship. In an effort to build the golfing strength of the Club the Captain, Cyril Hodkinson, asked the Board in 1947 to consider the formation of a colts' section to encourage the members in their early 20s. The Board supported his proposal and the decision was taken to arrange for each colt to receive ten lessons from the professional John Burton at the Club's expense. A Club Colts' Trophy, based on the best four cards submitted, was instituted. A Liverpool and District Colts' Challenge Cup had been introduced in 1934. This was an initiative to provide competitive golf for 18 to 28-year-olds who were unable to break into scratch teams. This competition lapsed during the war and was only revived in 1956, but it was to be 1965 before Hillside had a team strong enough to participate.

From 1925, a tradition of internal captain's team matches was developed. Captain's versus vice-captain's team matches were followed by a hot-pot supper and smoking concert. Social club matches continued to be played with the YMCA club; home and away fixtures were played in 1924.

Fig.62 *Society of Liverpool Golf Club Captains. The 'red coats' at their annual dinner.*

Other club matches were taken on over the years; a match has been played with Prenton since the 1940s, matches with close neighbour Royal Birkdale were played in the 1950s, and there was a regular fixture with S&A, occasional matches, including a 60-a-side fixture, having been played earlier. There were later about six captain's matches each year and at the subsequent dinner the result would be deemed 'an honourable draw'.

Club matches included one unusual fixture with the London Midland and Scottish Railway Company. Louis Rowlandson, the Hillside chairman, served this Company for 46 years and was its superintendent of organization and staff. The finals of the LMS Championship, which he initiated, were played annually at Hillside (Fig.63). From small beginnings the competition, which was open to employees in all grades and also to ladies, grew to attract almost 400 competitors. Eric Hawkins, later an active golfer at Hillside, won the championship in 1936. From 1928 Rowlandson was also responsible for an annual match between Hillside and an LMS team. These were matches with a result and John Hepburn, the 1935 captain of the Club, provided a silver putter as a team trophy. Rowlandson retired from the LMS in 1946, and in the following year the fixture was discontinued for lack of support. The redundant putter was presented to the Ladies' Section.

Fig.63 *Presentation at the annual London Midland and Scottish Railways Championship. This championship was played regularly at Hillside.*

Southport Infirmary Trophy

Started in 1933 by Paul Carter, a Councillor and the current captain of S&A, this competition was initiated to raise funds to endow beds at Southport Infirmary. It was open to all the Southport clubs and each played a qualifying competition, on the same day, with the entry fees going into the fund. Four players from each participating club qualified for the final and the club with the best three scores won the Paul Carter Silver Salver. The finals were hosted by Hillside in 1940 and again in 1945, when the home team was the winner. The introduction of the National Health Service in 1947 led to the winding up of this local competition, which had raised over £3,500 since its inception. A minor local mystery concerns the present whereabouts of the salver.

Southport Golf Week

In an attempt to encourage visitors to the town, the Southport Corporation decided to mount an annual golf week for amateurs. It was held in the week following the Flower Show, with the intention of extending the holiday season. It was another T.E. Wolstenholme initiative. A varied programme of competitions was offered on the resort's four major courses; the clubs received £25 from the Corporation for hosting one of these events. The week concluded with a presentation dance at the Floral Hall. In 1950, the inaugural year, 62 prizes with a value of £300 were awarded. As a further incentive to competitors they were issued with tickets to play a practice round on courses where they were due to compete.

The event proved to be very popular, particularly with local golfers (Fig.64), but as the fundamental purpose of the golf week was to attract visitors to the town, the Corporation officials attempted to adjust the regulations. Practice round facilities for local players were reduced, and then withdrawn and some of the prizes were restricted to visitors. The week continued to be popular, but local players were still the principal supporters. In spite of the adjustments to the regulations, the basic attraction remained – the opportunity for cheap competitive golf on the town's four major courses. The clubs lost their enthusiasm for the event and it was discontinued in 1957.

Fig.64 *Southport Golf Week 1954. Ladies waiting to drive from the first tee.*

The principal prizes were the Southport Bowls, one each for the ladies and gentlemen. In 1952 Frances Smith (Bunty Stephens) of Royal Birkdale won the trophy and in doing so set a course record at Hillside for the third time. Hillside's Charlie Blackshaw (Junior) won the men's bowl in 1950.

Hillside Ladies - with Pauline Horner

By 1923 ladies were allowed to play on Saturdays, but if the men had a competition, ladies couldn't go out until the men had all started. Lists of the winners of early Club competitions at Hillside include a predominance of unmarried ladies. In 1924, as the section was full, the Board decided that there should be no further 'unattached' lady members. The issue of female membership taxed many golf clubs at this time. It appears that the majority of men preferred it to be restricted to their wives and families. A harsh judgement when so many potential husbands had perished on the fields of Flanders.

The relationship between the leadership of the Ladies' Section and the Board was not good, and there appears to have been a strong personal dimension within this tension. Jessie Hargreave, who was decribed in the Board's minutes as the 'Ladies' Captain' rather than as the 'Lady Captain', was affronted when the Chairman's wife was asked to make a presentation that she felt she should have made, and she and her family subsequently resigned from the Club. Despite the fact that the Ladies' Section had paid for the building of a four-sided shelter on the course in 1923, the Board had been dissatisfied with aspects of how the leadership of the ladies was running the section and the ladies were required to draw up a new constitution and rules, which had to be approved by the Board. Under the leadership of the new Lady Captain, Mrs Ferguson, the reforms were in place by 1925 and a committee of the Lady Captain, the Vice Captain and five members was formalised. One of its early decisions was the purchase of five card tables, which became invaluable for hosting fund raising bridge and whist drives. The ladies asked that the section should be allowed to become a member of the Lancashire Ladies' County Golf Association, which had been formed in 1900. The financially pressed Board agreed to this request, but insisted that it should not involve the Club in any cost. From 1926 the ladies also conformed to the standards of the Ladies' Golf Union and sent delegates to its Annual Council.

The Lady Captain in 1926 and 1927 was Mrs Bon Bernard; she was an accomplished pianist who accompanied performers at Club fund-raising concerts, and she also looked after floral displays in the clubhouse. Her husband, a bank manager, was a Club committee member. The Committee of the Ladies' Section had a limited remit, but undertook its duties enthusiastically (Fig.65). From 1927 two lady members served on the Club's House Committee. In 1931 the ladies held both an invitation day and an open day. The Michelin Tyre Company sponsored the latter. To the satisfaction of the Board the ladies continued to organise a profitable Ladies' Annual Open Day, which included medal and foursomes rounds, along with driving and putting competitions (Fig.66).

Membership of the Lancashire Association provided the opportunity for Hillside members to compete outside the confines of club competitions. In 1926 Miss Nan Hunt, probably the section's strongest golfer, entered the county's Lady Derby Challenge Cup, a trophy presented by county president Lady

Fig.65 *'Ladies' Committee - early years.'* No other details are known about this labelled photograph in the Club scrapbook. It does not appear to have been taken at Hillside.

Fig.66 *Ladies' Open 1933. It is interesting to note that there were about a dozen men supporting this event.*

Alice Stanley and first played for in 1912. Miss Dorothy Aveyard, who was to serve as both honorary secretary and lady captain, reached the finals of this competition in 1931.

In 1926 an early season invitation foursomes competition was introduced by the fashionable ladies' periodical *Eve and Bystander*, which was taken by the Ladies' Section. Although *Eve* Ladies' Northern Counties' Foursomes Competition was a handicap event it attracted some of the country's outstanding golfers. In its early years Southport's three other major clubs hosted the event and, despite the participation of some 'stars', the majority of the competitors were modestly handicapped (Fig.67). Hillside members took part and a feature was that all the competitors received the much-prized *Eve* gift of a box of bon-bon chocolates.

The Club did not have a team powerful enough to compete in the County's Inter-Club Scratch Championship Shield, but a nine-strong Hillside team, led by Miss Nan Hunt and Miss E.A. Lawrenson, played in a friendly game against Morecambe Golf Club, handsomely winning the match. The Board also gave permission for a match with S&A ladies. The number of these informal matches grew. A County Handicap Shield was established in 1928 and in the following year the Club entered a team. By 1936 the team was strong enough to win five out of its eight matches, coming joint second with Hesketh. In this year the finals were played at Hillside. The team members were selected automatically based upon handicaps and any lady who won five of her eight matches in a season was entitled to wear a club badge a matching tie was later introduced. Three years later the team won seven of its eight matches and Hillside again tied with Hesketh. The outbreak of World War II prevented the finals from being played.

Within the Club there was an expanding golfing calendar and, from 1930 a ladies' fixture list was printed. The **Lady Captain's Prize** was first contested in 1922. Further trophies for new competitions - the **Sherrington Bowl** and the **Smith Cup** - were donated by George Sherrington (1924), Mr J.W. Smith (1926) and up until 1947 the winners received silver replicas. A prize for the **Best Scratch Score** was given by Miss Edie Buckley (1931). Silver spoons were given to medal winners. The needs of business members were recognised and they could enter major competitions if they could play before 6.30pm. Card play-offs were introduced in 1927 to save the contenders having to play a further 18 holes.

During the 1930s Miss Mary Berry twice won the Smith Cup, which had become a 36 holes competition in 1928. She received congratulations at the AGM for having reduced her handicap to 18. The question of handicap had become an important issue for the ladies. Handicap reductions were encouraged by the award of a prize at the AGM for the greatest annual reduction. The number of annual reductions was carefully recorded. A rule was introduced which dictated that any lady who won more than three prizes had to play off half-handicap until such time as she reduced. At the AGM in 1934 it was reported that there had been 32 reductions of handicap in the year and that the majority of ladies had handicaps under 25.

Fig.67 *The Eve Ladies' Northern Counties Foursomes Competition at S&A 1929. The dress of local golfers on the first tee illustrates contemporary golfing fashion.*

By 1932 Nan Hunt had got her handicap down to ten. She was the first winner of the Best Scratch Score Trophy in 1931, a title she was to hold in four of the next five years, her best score being 81. She also won the Lady Captain's Prize in 1931 and the Sherrington Bowl in 1934. Other winners included Miss Dorothy Aveyard, who won the Lady Captain's Prize twice and the Smith Cup once, and Miss Gladys Plummer, who won the Lady Captain's Prize, and the Sherrington Bowl three times. Up to the outbreak of the war in 1939 only 30 per cent of the winners of these four competitions were married. One of the most successful of the married ladies was Mrs R. Fairhurst who was the first winner of the Sherrington Bowl, a match play competition with a qualifying medal round, in 1925. She repeated this feat two years later and she won the Smith Cup in the following year.

World War II was to have a considerable impact on the Club. By 1941 the number of Hillside ladies either employed on war work or serving in the forces was so great that there was not the minimum of six competitors required for Division One. The handicap limit had to be extended to 23 in order to make the division viable. The Best Scratch Score competition was suspended, but the other major competitions were contested. One member, Miss Gladys Plummer, who was a ten-handicap golfer pre-war, served in the forces for eight years and after returning to civilian life in 1947 became Lady Captain in 1951.

In 1948 the Club was invited to host the Lancashire Ladies' Golf Association's annual championship for the first time. The title was won by Miss Frances (Bunty) Stephens, of Birkdale and she set a new ladies' record for the Hillside course during the qualifying stages. In 1949 the county side played at Hillside for the first time and the visitors – Durham – were comprehensively beaten. The English Ladies' County Finals were played at Hillside in 1955 and, after winning their semi-final against Gloucestershire, the Lancashire team was soundly beaten in the final by Surrey (Fig.68). In 1959 Hillside was again host to the Lancashire Championship, when Mrs Smith (Bunty Stephens) secured her ninth title.

The Club finally hosted the *Eve* Ladies' Northern Counties' Foursomes Competition in 1953. Five of the eight semi-finalists were from other Southport clubs and although we have no record of the rest of the field, it is highly likely that it included competitors from the home club. It was an event that brought further success to Bunty Stephens. Bunty obviously enjoyed playing at Hillside and had a long association with the Club. She was the daughter of Fred Stephens, the professional at the Bootle Municipal course, and started playing the game as a 12-year-old schoolgirl before the war. Her father brought her to play at Hillside and one former captain recalled seeing this 'slip of a girl', driving off the men's competition tees. During the war she regularly paid winter visits to Birkdale and became a member there in 1945 at the age of 21. Bunty frequently played with Robert Halsall, the Birkdale professional, and Hillside's John Burton. Although she became one of the all-time greats of ladies' golf she apparently achieved her first prize, a much cherished pickle jar, in a mixed foursome competition at Hillside.

Mrs Eileen Bankes, whose handicap was as low as four, dominated post-war club golf at Hillside. Between 1947 and 1967 she won the Best Scratch Score Trophy 15 times, with a lowest score of 74. She was Lady Captain in 1954 and acquired

Fig.68 *English Ladies' County Finals at Hillside 1955. The Lancashire Team: Frances (Bunty) Smith (Stevens) second from the right on the front row.*

the reputation for encouraging and helping other golfers with their game. She won the Lady Captain's Prize on three occasions, and the Sherrington Bowl and the Smith Cup once each. Other leading lady golfers at this time were Mrs Mabel Hawkins, four times winner of the Best Scratch score, and Mrs Lynne Moores who won it five times.

As with the men, John Burton encouraged ladies to participate in the Liverpool and District Golf Alliance. In the early 1930s Burton and Nan Hunt won mixed foursome competitions at Huyton, S&A and Hillside. In 1947, Eileen Bankes and Burton won the Nelson Cup, a trophy for a mixed foursome competition, which was donated in 1935. This was followed by his partnership with Mrs Clarice Hoyle, a two-time winner of Hillside's Best Scratch Score Trophy, and they won the Nelson Cup in three consecutive years. Their reign was brought to an abrupt end by the combination of Birkdale's Bunty Stevens and Bobby Halsall. Nevertheless Burton had been part of a winning combination on eight occasions.

Fig.69 *England Boys' Team, Royal Aberdeen 1935. Richard Rook, Hillside's first international, standing rear right.*

After the war, during which ladies in the services and working in industry had become accustomed to wearing slacks, there was a wish to use such practical form of clothing when playing golf. The LGU were strongly opposed to such a move and in 1963 the Hillside Board expressed its concern about lady members wearing them. Nevertheless the genie was out of the bottle and in their ever-evolving forms they have become an accepted form of dress. From 1969 ladies were permitted to wear trouser suits in the clubhouse.

County competitions were resumed after the war. The ladies' section briefly attempted to compete for the Inter-Club Scratch Championship Shield in the mid-1950s but soon withdrew and was represented only by a team in the Handicap Shield. In 1962 this team battled its way through to the finals at Wilpshire, where they lost in the final by only one match. There was an appetite for team golf beyond this format and friendly seven-a-side games for ladies with handicaps between 20 and 30 were instituted with Royal Birkdale and Formby Ladies.

Temporary Honorary Membership

In 1939, the Club established a practice of offering one-year temporary honorary membership to golfers from other local clubs, who had won major championships. The first went to Hesketh's Bentley brothers; Harold had won the English Amateur Championship in 1936 and Arnold in 1939, the year in which Harold won the Lancashire County title. Temporary honorary membership was also extended to Jackie Wroe when he won the Lancashire Championship in 1951. To mark her reign as Open and Lancashire Champion in 1954, Hillside extended honorary membership to Bunty Stephens, who never lost a singles' game in her six consecutive Curtis Cup matches against the USA.

Juniors

It was a junior member who brought Hillside its first international golfing honour. Richard Rook (Junior), whose father and mother had achieved a notable family double in 1932 by winning the Captain's Prize and the Lady Captain's Prize respectively, and whose sister Pam was later to emulate her mother and win the Lady Captain's Prize in 1948 and 1949, played in the British Boys' Championship at Royal Aberdeen in 1935 and was selected to play for England Boys against Scotland Boys (Fig.69). Richard had joined the Club as an 11-year-old in 1929. Although they were not allowed to play in other Club competitions, Pam and Richard won a mixed foursomes competition.

Charlie Blackshaw (Junior), the son of a member, joined the Club as a junior in 1930. In 1936 the British Boys' Championship was played at Birkdale and Charlie distinguished himself by losing a closely contested semi-final to Irishman James (the Loop) Bruen, who went on to win the Championship and to become a legendary amateur player. Two local schoolboy internationals, Ronnie White (Birkdale) and Tom Hiley (S&A), had already been eliminated from this championship; whilst a second Hillside junior, Jackie Wroe, was defeated in the first round.

Junior membership at Hillside was officially restricted to the sons of members, but the Club did little to encourage them. Pam Roberts (nee Rook) recalls that her brother played mostly with Charlie Blackshaw. Both had been admitted as members early, although the Club rules stated that juniors were unable to join the Club until they were 14-years-of-age when they were allowed to play at the weekend, subject to the same restrictions as the ladies. By 1939 both boys were playing off a handicap of three. Walter Wilkinson, whose father was a member and the builder of the clubhouse, joined as a 16-year-old in the 1930s. Gordon Hughes, another long-time Club member joined as a junior in 1949, when the annual subscription was one guinea (£1.05) and there was no entrance fee (Fig.70). In the mid-1940s the rules were amended and members' sons were officially allowed to join at the age of 11.

By the late 1930s the rules allowed non members' sons to become members, but the subscription was double that of the sons of members. Stuart Brown, a resident of Shore Road born in 1924 was a junior member '...for two or three years before the war', as was his friend John Bennett of Sandbrook Road.

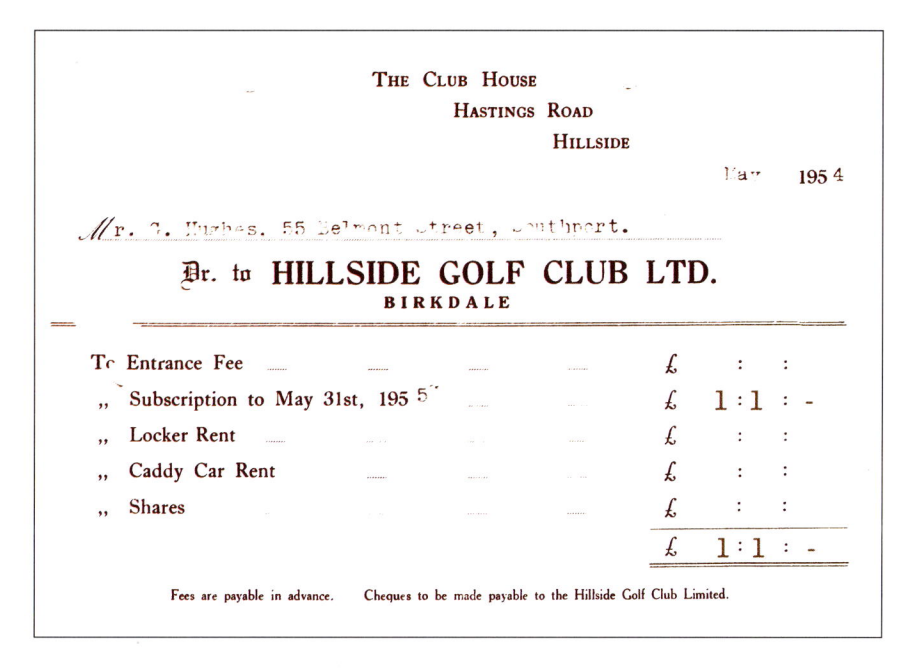

Fig.70 *Junior Membership Fee Receipt 1954.*

Both were pupils at Bickerton House School in Birkdale Park and neither were the sons of members. The boys were not involved in any Club activities; they paid their annual fee and '...tried to keep out of the way', mostly playing on the four holes at the Ainsdale end of the course. Harold James became a junior member in 1946 and paid his initial subscription from his earnings as a butcher's boy delivering orders. He was proposed for membership by Club Captain Ben Turner and seconded by Mrs Elizabeth Berry, the local butcher who employed him and who later dragooned him to play with her in the Bank Holiday Mixed Foursomes. There was still no formally organised junior section but Harold recalls a number of members who coached him and one who instructed him on the rules and etiquette of the game. He did his mentors proud being selected for the Lancashire Boys' team and in 1954 for a Lancashire Colts' team match against Cheshire at Hillside. He played for this team for a further two years. Another junior whose parents were not members was Ainsdale boy Tony Coop, who joined the Club in 1949. Tony had not been allowed to join S&A because he was a part-time caddie there. When he left school he became an assistant to Jim Gerrard, the professional at Hesketh Golf Club. Juniors at Hillside continued, however, to be principally the children of members. The attitude of the Board to junior membership was revealed in its minutes which, in 1961, included the following statement: 'Children of other than members are not to be encouraged due to the difficulty of assessing character.'

The daughters of members had been allowed membership in a similar fashion to the boys, although when the age for boys was reduced to 11 that for girls officially remained at 14. It seems

Fig.71 *Annual Dinner 1933. A group of Hillside and visiting captains. Hillside Captain W.R.H. Gibbs seated 3rd right, to his right L.F. Rowlandson, standing from the left: J.M.T. Reynolds, 6th, M.E. Bishop, 7th, A. Poirrette, 8th and H.S. Collinge, 9th.*

likely that only a few girls played, Pam Roberts (Rook), who was allowed to join as an 11-year-old in 1932, cannot recall any other active girl members.

From the 1960s Hillside began to take more account of the welfare of younger members. Rules and conditions were formulated for their participation and they received letters '...setting out what is expected of them.' Previously it was the ladies' section which organised an annual competition for the juniors during the school holidays. By this time their number had risen to over 40 and the ladies asked the Board if this boys' event could be supervised by the men. A junior section was formally established in 1958 with the captain Bill Rayner accepting responsibility and he arranged lessons for the juniors with John Burton. By 1965, Fred Wormold and Gordon Rimmer had taken on the role of junior organisers. A programme of junior competitions was put in place and, with the support of the Golf Foundation, group lessons were given to younger members, including girls. Membership for girls was still restricted to members' daughters and there were few of them. The Board did accede to a request from the ladies to admit up to six girls, whose parents were not members, but this concession had little take up.

In 1960 the Southport and District Perpetual Boys' Challenge Trophy was presented by a past captain of Hesketh in an attempt to promote junior golf in the district. Brian Whittle, a KGV boy who had joined Hillside in 1958, won this 36 holes handicap competition for boys between the ages of 11 and 17 in 1961. Brian went on to become an assistant to professional Ted Jarman at the West Lancashire Club, before moving to a post in Scandinavia.

Social Affairs

The Club's social calendar was expanded and refined during this period. Photographs show that the annual dinner was in place by 1933 (Fig.71), whilst an annual dinner dance was held at the Birkdale Palace Hotel as early as 1923, by 1934

Fig.72 *Annual Dinner Dance, Prince of Wales Hotel 1952.*

it was held at the Prince of Wales Hotel (Fig.72). The Captain's year that had previously run from August, was changed to a January 1st start in 1936, giving the opportunity for the now traditional New Year's Day drive in.

The onset of war in 1939 quickly had an impact on the finances of the Club. Income was affected by the shortage of supplies of alcohol and cigarettes, and overall there was a dramatic drop in revenue. In the absence of staff, in the forces or on war work, members looked after the bar. Two future captains, Ben Turner and George Ball regularly fulfilled the role. Lady members assisted with the serving of teas and other clubhouse tasks. One beneficial effect of these arrangements was the consequent reduction in labour costs which helped the Club to balance its books through these difficult years.

The courtesy of the course was extended to visiting members of His Majesty's Forces, merchant seamen and allied servicemen. The majority of those who availed themselves of this concession were American airmen staying at Birkdale's requisitioned, and now demolished, Palace Hotel, whilst having a break from flying bombing missions over Europe (Fig.73). Naval personnel from HMS Queen Charlotte, the training unit for maritime gunners, based on the Lido at the top of Shore Road, Ainsdale, were also regular visitors. Many of these servicemen were golfing novices and inflicted considerable damage on the course. A new category of Civil Service Membership was introduced for civil servants whose departments had been evacuated from London to Southport to work in one of the town's requisitioned hotels.

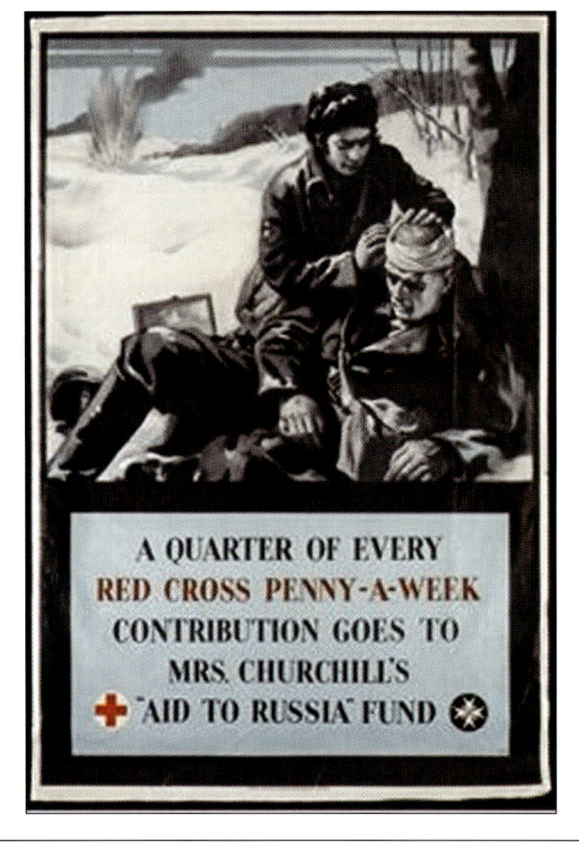

Shortages of coal, jam and marmalade are noted in the minutes of the Ladies' Committee. During the war the ladies raised over £400 for various war charities (Fig.74). This was achieved by holding a 'Charity Day' each month and organizing regular bridge and whist drives.

The Club celebrated the end of hostilities VE (Victory in Europe) and VJ (Victory in Japan) by replacing the normal flags on the greens with Union Jacks and offering members a free drink. A Victory Dinner was later arranged.

In 1948 the first children's Christmas Party took place. Successive captains regarded this event as an important way of encouraging the youngsters to become 'golf-club minded' in order that they may become future members of the Club. This annual party was allowed to lapse, but was revived in 1963 and was organised by the Ladies' Section. A New Year's Eve dance, with a limit of 100, was introduced in 1950. By the 1960s the formal annual club dinner had lapsed but was later reinstated in the enlarged dining room.

Caddies, mainly schoolboys, were still a feature of club life after the war, but what were originally called 'auto caddies' (trolleys) were introduced in the late 1940s (Fig.75).

Fig. 75 An 'auto-caddie' on the first tee c.1948. This trolley is said to be the first to be used at Hillside. It had a rigid frame and narrow wheels.

Fig.73 (Top Left). American Red Cross Service Club, Palace Hotel 1942-1945. A bomber crew in front of the entrance. This was the largest American Red Cross facility in this country. In addition to extending the courtesy of their golf courses, the local clubs provided golf equipment for the airmen.

Fig.74 (Botton Left). A poster for Mrs Churchill's Aid to Russia Fund. This was one of the war charities supported by the Hillside Ladies. A cheque for £47 was sent in October 1941 and a further £65 in 1943

Chapter Seven
A Championship Course
1967 - 2010

The Guardians

From 1967 to 1971 Freddie Veale was the Club Chairman. The era of Hillside's authoritarian chairmen, Rowlandson, Poirrette and Collinge, who had managed to save the faltering club from possible oblivion, had passed and the mantle had fallen on a gentler man, a man more at ease with the members.

Veale, a native of North Wales, had been a member of Childwall Golf Club and joined Hillside as a country member in 1936 and, although still living in Woolton, he became a full member in 1945, captain in 1953 and chairman between 1967 and 1971. His generosity to the Club is legendary, and he was made an Honorary Life Member in 1971. In addition to his service to Hillside as a captain, chairman and committee man, he was a vice president of the North Region of the PGA, and a president of the Liverpool Alliance. In recognition of his contributions, the PGA presented him with a silver salver in 1977 (Fig.76). From 1986 this became the Freddie Veale Salver for an 18 holes handicap competition. It was typical of the man that when volunteers were required for the tasks involved in Hillside becoming a qualifying course for the Open Championship, he took on the role of chief steward. Those who remember Freddie will think not of the offices that he held but of the amiable man, who, in his advancing years, would regularly go for a cup of tea and a chat in the professional's shop followed by a walk as far as the 4th tee before returning to the clubhouse.

Fig.76 *Presentation to Freddie Veale by the Northern Section of the PGA 1977. John McAlister, the Captain is second from the left.*

During the critical period of the Club's history, from 1923 until the 1960s, the executive power of the chairmanship had rested in few hands and there had been continuity in the discharge of the office. The three long-serving chairmen who preceded Veale had served for 13, 12 and 14 years respectively, whilst the next 14 averaged two and a half years' tenure with only two serving for more than four years.

The change evident in the tenure of the chairmen appears to have been reflected in the choice of captains. Before 1962 when Bert Collinge, who had previously been captain in 1931, served a second term, there were eight other Hillside captains who served at least two terms and as many as five. Since then, no captain has been nominated to serve for more than one year.

As Southport Corporation was the landowner of the course, Local Government Re-organisation in 1974 was to have a profound impact on the Club. Southport, an independent county borough, along with Bootle County Borough and parts of Lancashire County were to be merged into a new Metropolitan Borough of Sefton. Sefton was to be a second tier authority of an over-arching Merseyside County Council. Decision-making was going to take place a long way from Southport town hall, which had forged such strong links with the local golf clubs. Before this re-organisation took place Southport Corporation offered to re-negotiate the leases with its three tenant golf clubs. The opportunity to replace Hillside's existing two nines lease (99 years) with a new three nines lease, and thus secure the Club's long-term future was seized. This 999 years lease provided for a fixed rent for 60 years, with rent reviews every 21 years thereafter. As the years passed the uncertainties associated with the future rent reviews encouraged the Board to enter negotiations with the Corporation in an attempt to purchase the freehold. This initiative failed, but the Club did secure a rent review buy out. For the payment of a substantial fee to the Council, in the year 2000, future rent reviews were bought out and the rent was retained at the original figure for the remainder of the lease. Sefton's other two golf course tenants - Royal Birkdale and Hesketh - made similar prudent purchases.

In the late 1990s the 'e' word – equality – became common currency in clubhouse conversations. Despite the presence of lady members, golf clubs had long been male bastions with ladies having the status of second class citizens. Hillside had been no exception to this general practice. But by 1998 the Board was holding meetings with representatives of the Ladies' Section and considering a discussion paper on the rights of ladies within the Club. Concern was growing about the implications of the impending Sex Discrimination Act, which was due to follow the European inspired Human Rights Act of 1998. At Hillside, as elsewhere, there was anxiety about the attitude and possible actions of the licensing authority. Golf clubs had to have a Club Registration Certificate that was subject to periodic renewal. Amongst the existing conditions was a requirement that no section of the membership should be without a vote in the conduct of the Club. This had been so since the Licensing Act of 1964, but had been largely ignored by golf clubs and the licensing authority. A new impetus to achieve equality had come with the election of a Labour government in 1997, with a manifesto commitment to outlaw all forms of discrimination. Golf clubs, fearful of losing their licence to sell alcohol, urgently addressed the issue. At Hillside, after some 'cosmetic' concessions concerning clubhouse access had been made, the nettle was firmly grasped in 2001 when it was decided that lady members could be shareholders with voting rights. Full lady members had previously had to hold two shares, as opposed to the five held by men, but they had no voting rights. The Lady Captain became an ex-officio member of the Board and its committees and was to give an annual report on the Ladies' Section at the Club's AGM (Fig.77).

Fig.77 *Historic AGM, December 2001. From the left: lady captain elect Jean Hough, captain elect George Charnock, Lady Captain Ann Turnbull, Captain Ian McDiarmid and chairman Gary Taylor.*

In her report to the AGM in 2003, the Lady Captain pointed out that no lady had yet been elected to the Board. Geraldine Evans had the distinction of becoming the first lady to achieve this status in 2006. Sadly she died one year later. A second lady director, Mrs Barbara Anderson the Lady Captain of 2007, was elected in 2008 and by 2010 the female presence on the Board was up to three.

The Course

The course is a golf club's principal asset and Hillside's had undergone extensive development. This reconstruction had been made possible by the innovative and imaginative co-operation between Southport County Borough, the landowner, and Hillside Golf Club, the tenant. The exchange of some of the land that was leased to the Club was mutually beneficial, whilst the sale of sand paid for improvements that would have been beyond the capacity of the Club to finance. The reconstructed course was officially opened on the 1st July 1967, when lunch was provided for invited guests followed by champagne served on the 1st tee prior to a members' four ball better ball competition (Fig.78). Aubrey Fawcett and Barry Whiteside were the winners.

Amendments continued to be made to the course. The course, like so many of its contemporaries, lacked an adequate practice ground, a facility that was becoming an essential requirement for major tournaments. For many years practice had been confined to the 16th (now the 9th) fairway, and it was here that John Burton gave lessons. In order to provide a dedicated practice ground, the Corporation allowed the Club an additional area of land, between the 18th fairway and Royal Birkdale's 18th, but a gap had got to be left between the two courses for a public right of way, which became a popular dog-walking path. The new practice ground was brought into use in 1968, along with a new putting green. In the following year Ted MacAvoy, the head greenkeeper successfully suggested the insertion of a pond on the right of the 12th fairway thus defining its dogleg shape (Fig.79). Its presence also helped to alleviate the drainage problem in this low-lying area. The ditch running across the fairway in front of the 3rd green had been put into a culvert in a porous pipe in 1968 and in 1971 it was re-opened and flagged.

Fig.78 *Opening the new course 1967. From the left: Freddie Veale (Chairman), John Burton, Captain Bill Sawyer and Bert Collinge (former chairman and chairman of green).*

During 1971 another 4,000 trees were planted '...to give finish to the course.' Further planting was later used to replace trees lost to Dutch Elm disease. A national 'Plant a Tree Year' was designated in 1973 and the Board invited members to make donations for trees. Chestnut, Laburnum, Sycamore and Silver Birch were planted, none of which were dune land trees and some would later regard them as undesirable alien introductions.

In 1971 a new 10th hole was constructed. This short hole had previously been played to a small plateau green, from which steep artificially uniform slopes fell away on all sides. To the right of the old green a new two-level green was cut deep into the pinewood clad sandhills, with a narrow approach, which was guarded by deep bunkers (Fig.80). Some 80 trees had to be removed. John Burton and Ted MacAvoy had a considerable input into the design of this hole.

Fig.79 *Putting out on the 12th green 1989. The dog-leg swept around the lake on the left. Spoil from excavation of the lake was tipped to form the tall bank at its rear.*

MacAvoy was not only a good greenkeeper but was also a competent golfer. He was actively involved in the Greenkeepers' Association and competed successfully in its golf competitions, winning the national championship in 1963. Totally committed to his work at Hillside, he was largely responsible for keeping the course available for golf during the reconstruction and speedily bringing areas into play, albeit with restrictions. Sadly in 1972 he died in the greenkeepers' shed. In recognition of his services to the Club he had previously been made an honorary member. Subsequently a memorial **MacAvoy Trophy** was presented for competition within the Club, by his brother George, and was awarded for the first time in 1974.

In 1968, after the completion of the major course reconstruction, the Club considered installing a pop-up irrigation system. Existing provision had been from wells, with the water being abstracted by pumps mounted on trailers for labour intensive hand-held hose spraying. Although there was widespread support for the irrigation initiative and tenders were received, financial difficulties led to it being shelved. It was in 1971, Freddie Veale's last year as Chairman, that he offered the Club an interest free loan for the installation of an automatic sprinkler system. Costs were pared by the Club's staff undertaking the excavation of trenches, using a hired 'mole' plough. They also completed the restoration of the ground. The system was partial and did not cover the entire course. Veale gave a further £3,000 in 1975 for a limited extension of the system. Water was extracted from the lake alongside the 3rd green and there was a low capacity tank for the storage of mains water by the car park.

With the approach of the millennium the Board decided to take stock of its assets and to formulate a strategic plan to meet future challenges – 'A Business Plan for the Course Management and Development of Hillside Golf Course.' Irrigation was identified as the most pressing problem. The existing system did not give complete coverage of the course and was wasteful compared to an up-to-date system, at a time when water was becoming a precious and expensive commodity. In 1999 the R&A funded a research programme into water resource requirements of golf courses on the Sefton coast. Although all the Hillside greens received water only five fairways had any coverage. A system, costing some £300,000, was installed to give full cover for all greens, tees, fairways, approaches and walk-offs. The pop-up sprinklers were radio controlled from a computer terminal in the maintenance

Fig.80 *The 10th hole. The new green is set in the dunes, through the gap in the pines. The former plateau green was still in use. The tee was being extended.*

sheds. The system was fed from a 36 feet diameter tank in the trees to the left of the 9th fairway, which was linked to the pond alongside the 3rd green. The contractor warned, however, that grains of sand from this reservoir lake could get into the system and possibly cause the sprinkler heads to stick. Like neighbours Royal Birkdale and Southport and Ainsdale, Hillside had experienced difficulties with sediment from the reservoir lake clogging pump filters and damaging pipe work. Trespassing boys fishing had eroded the banks of the lake and the resulting subsidence had exacerbated the problem. The other two clubs had replaced their existing lake water extraction systems with linear well point systems, which were laid in the dune sand aquifer. Hillside decided to follow this example and a 280 metre long pipe was installed at a depth of 4.5 metres between the 1st and 2nd and the 9th fairways in November 2004 (Fig.81). The pump was installed in an extension of the original pump house alongside the pond.

In these environmentally sensitive times such projects cannot be undertaken without extensive consultation with the relevant agencies. In addition to the fauna familiar to members, such as rabbits and red squirrels (recently decimated by squirrelpox virus), the course is an important habitat for threatened species such as natterjack toads and sand lizards; whilst the flora includes grey hair grass and the nationally rare dune helleborine. The course had been designated a Site of Biological Important Status and any major work in such Special Areas of Conservation is subject to careful consideration of its potential impact. In this scheme there had to be no undue damage to any of the water dependant nature conservation features. Decisions lay with the Environment Agency, but the Club also has to meet the concerns of English Nature and the Sefton Environmental Advisory Agency. For example in order to ensure that sand lizard friendly habitats are preserved, the Club had to appoint a consultant from the Herpetological Conservation Trust.

The sand lizard is the most threatened of our three native lizard species and is subject to English Nature's Species Recovery Programme, as the Sefton dune coast is one of the few locations where this reptile survives, and is the most northerly. The sand lizard is Britain's only egg laying lizard and needs areas of open sand on sunny banks to incubate eggs. Any disturbance of the dunes during construction had to take account of the lizards. It is only in the summer breeding season when sand lizards are active that you might catch a glimpse of one of these elusive creatures before it scurries away. They live in colonies and tend not to move around, making them easier to find. For six months of the year they hibernate, living in a state of torpor in their burrows. Natterjack toads bred on the course up until the late 1980s and efforts have been made to reinstate their presence. The perception that golf courses and wild life do not mix and that golf courses are sterile artificially manicured playgrounds is dying. Hillside now takes its responsibilities towards conservation very seriously and, stimulated by articles and illustrations in *Hillside Links*, members are becoming more aware of the environment they share with diverse plant and animal populations.

Fig.81 *Installing the Horizontal Well Point System 2004. This machine was digging the trench whilst the operative fed the extraction pipe into the boom to be laid into the trench.*

After a rigorous consultation process with the relevant agencies the Club was granted a five-year water abstraction licence in 2005. Using the new system the volume of water, which the Club was allowed to extract annually, was increased almost threefold. The water levels in the ground are strictly monitored as is the amount abstracted. The Club has to pay a fee to the Environment Agency for this water.

Fig.82 *Tall bank alongside the railway behind the 5th green.*

Hillside's back nine, with its monumental 'new' holes, had consistently attracted praise. The front nine holes, principally on the flatter land of the 1923 course, suffered by comparison. In the millennium year it was decided to have a professional course review, with a view to upgrading them. Donald Steel, the eminent golf journalist and course architect, was retained to produce a 'frank' report on the course. In his appraisal he acknowledged the contrast between the two halves, but his overall impression was that Hillside was the '…hardest course in England with a card and a pencil in your hand' but he applauded the fact that it did not suffer from a surfeit of bunkers and identified the wind as its strongest protection.

He argued that the layout of the course should recognise the impact of the rapid rate of improvement that had occurred in the manufacture of golf equipment. Principally there was a need to 'rearrange the furniture', particularly the fairway bunkers. They, he maintained, should pose problems to the good players, but those that only trapped indifferent players should be filled in. He also had suggestions to make in relation to greenside bunkers.

Steel also thought that it in some places the Hillside course was not '…as aesthetically pleasing as it might be.' He identified a surprising number of old banks and greens that littered the course. He argued that they had no utility and in his view were ugly eyesores in a links' landscape. One of the most blatant examples of this clutter was the tall symmetrical bank alongside the railway fence by the green on the 5th hole (Fig.82). This artificial looking feature had been built in the 1960s to shield the green from the railway. Another example was the former plateau green on the short 10th hole (see Fig.80).

Having made his report Steel was employed to supervise work on the course at a final cost close to £100,000. The 5th hole experienced the most extensive make over in the revisions. Fairway bunkers were re-arranged to challenge the drive of better players. The hole formerly required a blind shot to the green over a large sleeper-faced bunker in a col between two tall sand dunes. This bunker was removed thus opening up the view of the green from the fairway (Fig.83). Spoil from the redundant bank alongside the railway, the old 10th green and elsewhere was used to extend the two guarding sand dunes towards the green, with sympathetically shaped mounds and banks flanking either side of the narrow fairway. Other examples of the strategic repositioning of bunkers are evident on the 2nd, 4th and 14th holes, whilst a number of other holes have had their greenside bunkers reconfigured.

From 2001 the Club was part of the partnership for Sefton Coast Woodlands to help plan woodland development and maintenance. It is argued that if traditional links course are allowed, or encouraged, to develop into woodland they lose their special character. As at all the other clubs on this sand dune coast, the course architect was advocating the removal of ornamental trees, encroaching sycamore and white poplar trees and buckthorn, which he described as 'an insidious weed.' (At Hillside buckthorn has helped to maintain the vulnerable ill-defined western boundary.) He also wanted surviving trees managed in such a way that they did not threaten the light, air and water available on greens and tees. The removal of trees from the immediate vicinity of the 4th green is an example. As at other courses on the coast, such proposals proved contentious, the presence of trees on seaside links golf courses is an emotive issue. A compromise was secured and not all of Steel's recommendations were accepted, for example, the suggestion that the belt of conifers alongside the 1st fairway should be removed in order to restore the opening drive of a classic railway hole was rejected. However, cypresses and leylandii which had been planted in symmetrical rows, such as those between the 2nd and 9th holes, were removed and replaced with scattered pines (see Fig. 91).

The opportunity was also taken to address the drainage problems that had plagued the 2nd, 3rd and 12th holes. The ditch that brought water from the 12th hole across the 3rd fairway was reshaped. Before the linear well point water extraction system was installed, the pond on the 2nd hole was cleaned and deepened and a winding open ditch cut in front of the 2nd tee

Fig.83 *5th Hole 2008, approach to the green.*

across to the ditch alongside the railway fence, where another man-made bank was removed. It may seem odd but the lower-lying area of the course, by the railway, drained inland for the surplus water to make its way to the sea at Crossens to the north of Southport. The water left Hillside through a culvert under the railway track, and on in a ditch through the S&A course before entering the main drainage system. The silting of these intermediate channels, which were outside the control of the Club, continued to cause problems.

As the Hillside course was to be used for the Open Championship qualifying in 2001, the changes proposed by Steel were undertaken in phases and completed in two winter programmes. The greenkeeping staff, led by Martin Twist, were again able to deliver a massive contribution to course development.

Fig.84 *Fire ravaged course 2006. Looking across the 13th fairway.*

Disaster struck the course during the summer drought of 2006. Two pupils from Ainsdale Hope High School set fire to the tinder dry undergrowth behind their school. The blaze quickly spread to the rough at the margin of the adjoining 13th fairway. From here it crossed to the other side of the fairway and over the hill behind the green (Fig.84). The green staff switched on the irrigation system, and this along with the efforts of the local fire brigade, limited the amount of damage, but the scars from this act of vandalism lingered long.

Minor improvements continued to be made to the course. In 2009 the R&A requested that the practice ground be upgraded by the installation of a tee with a surface that would make it playable throughout the winter. The putting green was expanded towards the course in order to allow the paved terrace in front of the clubhouse to be extended.

The course continued to benefit from the Hillside tradition of members making gifts to the Club. Inscriptions on the starter's hut and on benches scattered about the course

Fig.85 *The halfway house 2010. The building has a pyramidal roof reminiscent of the original clubhouse and is nestled into a bank overlooking the 9th green. The path leads to the 10th tee.*

reveal such acts of philanthropy. More substantial is the brick-built 'halfway house' with its excellent facilities for respite and refreshment (Fig.85). A substantial bequest from the husband of Eileen Bankes, a distinguished past lady captain and golfer, covered some of the cost. Denis Nutter, a former chairman of green, specified that the money in his bequest should be spent on resurfacing the service road that runs through the course and is much used by the greenkeeping staff.

With the onset of the new millennium the Board held a fundamental review of the clubhouse and its facilities, attempting to assess the changing future needs and opportunities. It adopted a Business Plan with an ambitious agenda of goals, and a Development Committee was established. The Board advocated an attempt to integrate the disparate developments of the past, whilst addressing contemporary issues, such as access for the disabled and equality for lady members. The proposed make over was

The Clubhouse

Since the clubhouse was originally built in 1924, it had been developed with a series of extensions. Their purpose has included addressing social change and particular issues as they arose; for example the installation of the snooker room and the mixed cocktail lounge. This process had continued with the opening of a junior clubroom, at the front of the clubhouse in 1972. A further building programme was successfully proposed in the following year. This included improvements to the toilets and washroom, an extension of the ladies' locker room, and work on the spike bar. The locker room, trolley store and professional's shop were expanded and the gap between the clubhouse and the railway was closed. The car park was later re-ordered with the entrance and exit being brought up to modern security standards.

New showers and toilets for the men were installed in 1994. Four years later the men's lockers were replaced, using 'the VAT money'. In 1998 golf clubs were able to recover from the Inland Revenue money that it had incorrectly charged on members' subscriptions over many years in the form of Value Added Tax. At Hillside the Board successfully proposed that part of this windfall should be used to pay for a £90,000 scheme to renew the men's lockers. The new lockers were shorter than those they replaced and consequently the room had a lighter, more open, spacious appearance. In 2002 the ladies' powder room was refurbished.

Fig.86 *The foyer 2010. The view through the foyer extends into the lounge and to the course beyond. The re-aligned staircase, the corner of the reception counter and the trophy cabinet are in the foreground.*

intended to give the clubhouse a more coherent integrated appearance, a contemporary but distinctively Hillside look. Such a comprehensive, and necessarily expensive, undertaking could never hope to attract universal support in a members' club, but phased projects were put in place to successfully implement the scheme.

The initial phase of the development was started in 2004. A lift was installed giving wheelchair access from the foyer to the first floor, where toilets, including provision for the disabled, were fitted, using the former domestic accommodation. Some of this space was also used to provide a boardroom. On the ground floor, the secretary's office was relocated during this phase. Central to the second phase was the work undertaken on the entrance and foyer. A spacious porch with large windows is set at a right angle to the wide main foyer

paid for by George MacAvoy. The foyer has been transformed into an impressive light, open introduction to the clubhouse (Fig.86). The opportunity was taken to create a TV lounge annexe to the main lounge by using a corridor and the former cocktail bar, which had become something of a white elephant. Phase two included the refurbishment and refurnishing of all the communal areas, which have taken on the appearance of a planned integrated whole (Fig.87). The House Committee Chairman, described the renovated clubhouse as having '...a contemporary feel whilst retaining the traditions of Hillside Golf Club.'

Phase three should be completed prior to the centenary celebrations. It is proposed to build a larger shop for the professional, backing onto the railway and overlooking the 1st tee. The space released by this relocation will be used to enlarge the ladies' locker room. The small former trolley store will be incorporated into the mens' changing room. The terrace / patio area in front of the clubhouse will be enlarged and upgraded, whilst the buggy park will be re-located, beyond the professional's new shop, by the path alongside the 1st tee.

The officers of the Club and their committees, the 'Guardians', had overseen the development of a course and clubhouse that confirmed Hillside's status as a first-class championship course (Fig.88).

Fig.87 *Main lounge 2010. The fireplace had to be removed to create the new entrance from the foyer. To the right, beyond the entrance, the television lounge annexe is tucked away. Through the opening to the left of the bar is the spike bar.*

doors, which are flanked by glass panels. The wall formerly facing this threshold, which backed onto the fireplace in the main lounge, was removed and wide doors were installed thus creating a view across the foyer and lounge onto the course. The direction of the double flight staircase from the foyer to the first floor and the dining room was reversed and the staircase straightened into a single length. Outside the secretary's office is a reception desk, alongside which a handsome trophy cabinet has been built into the wall; this was

Fig.88 *(Overleaf) Card of the course 2005. The pyramidal roof of the original clubhouse surrounded by flat-roofed extensions.*

	Gentlemen		Ladies			Gentlemen		Ladies	
Hole	Yards	Par	Yards	Par	Hole	Yards	Par	Yards	Par
1	399	4	382	5	10	147	3	141	3
2	525	5	454	5	11	508	5	481	5
3	402	4	328	4	12	368	4	314	4
4	195	3	165	3	13	398	4	325	4
5	504	5	426	5	14	400	4	346	4
6	413	4	327	4	15	398	4	322	4
7	176	3	145	3	16	199	3	146	3
8	405	4	351	4	17	548	5	497	5
9	425	4	381	5	18	440	4	388	5
Out	3444	36	2959	38	In	3406	36	2960	37
					Out	3444	36	2959	38
					Total	6850	72	5919	75
					SSS		74		75

Chapter Eight
A Tournament Venue of Choice
1967 - 2010

Professional Tournaments

The new Hillside course was used for the PGA's four-round **Under 23 Professional Golf Tournament** in 1968. The PGA's president Lord Derby donated the prize fund of £1,200 and 21-years-old Guy Hunt, won the first prize of £150.

In 1971 the **Roosevelt Memorial Polio Fund Nine Nations Tournament**, a charity fund-raiser, was played at Hillside on the Sunday before the Open at Royal Birkdale. This annual tournament, inaugurated in 1964, attracted a strong field from those who did not have to qualify for the Open. Competitors at Hillside included the Argentinean former Open Champion Roberto de Vicenzo. The format had been revised and a two-man team represented each of the participating countries. Peter Thomson won the individual prize of £200, with a course record score of 65, and, as a member of the Australian team, along with Bruce Devlin, took a share of the team prize of £200.

Carreras, the tobacco company, returned to Hillside for its **Piccadilly Medal Match Play** event in 1972. Notable early victims included Tony Jacklin, winner of the Open and the US Open, and Peter Oosterhuis, who played in six Ryder Cup matches and is now a TV commentator based in America. Tommy Horton and Guy Hunt, competent competitors if not charismatic champions, contested the 36 holes final. The day was marred by heavy rain and strong winds and only a small crowd followed the event, and, as it was medal match play, it had to go the full 36 holes before Horton could be confirmed as winner of the £2,500 first prize.

The following year another tobacco company brought the **Benson and Hedges Match Play Tournament** to Hillside (Fig.89). The prize fund of £20,000 attracted a strong field including Tony Jacklin, Christie O'Connor, Peter Alliss, Bernard Gallagher, Peter Oosterhuis, Phil Rodgers and Neil Coles. Coles, who had won the event twice previously, took the first prize of £3,500. It was estimated that the daily attendance had exceeded 3,000 and the sponsor was highly satisfied.

Fig.89 *Benson and Hedges PGA Match Play Championship 1973.*

Attracted by golf's growing popularity, its image and its increasing exposure in the media, major international companies, particularly in the tobacco industry, were pouring money into golf tournaments. Hillside appeared to be following Royal Birkdale as one of the promoters' venues of choice for professional tournaments and the Club received substantial facility fees for hosting these events.

Tournament golf was, however, becoming big business and the PGA was under pressure from the leading tournament professionals to generate more income from it. They wanted the PGA to separate the administration of tournament golf from the more mundane day to day concerns of club professionals, something that had been achieved in America in 1968. In 1975, the British tournament professionals finally emulated their American counterparts and got their own separate division of the PGA. European Tour tournaments went to promoters who sought the credibility of celebrity for their events. The professionals and their association had discovered that the private promoters who had spent lavishly to produce a new generation of courses, frequently associated with hotels, or some form of property development, were willing to invest heavily to attract events, such as the increasingly popular Ryder Cup match, with its extensive television coverage. The entrepreneurs recognised the commercial power of image by association and the PGA had become aware that it had a valuable product to market. No longer did it offer a facility fee to a club for the use of its course, it sought payment from the venue. Tournaments appear to have been 'sold' to the highest bidder and they were invariably played on proprietary courses seeking to publicise these venues through the media coverage that the game was attracting.

These changes in the promotion of the professional game mean that the leading professionals seldom now play in tournaments at club courses such as Hillside. In 1982, the Club appeared to buck this trend in spectacular fashion when it hosted the **Sun-Alliance PGA Tournament**. It was suggested in the press that Hillside had been '…chosen for its excellence as a championship course.' Golf writer Louis Stanley, however, injected an air of reality and noted that '…it is nine years since a professional tournament has been staged here.'

It is this event that many remember as the high spot of Hillside's history as a professional tournament venue. It was preceded by a Pro-Am, which was won by the team led by Ryder Cup player and TV commentator Brian Barnes. On the first day of the tournament proper a fierce wind blowing over the 6,951 yards-long course proved to be a daunting challenge. Ryder Cup captain to be, Sam Torrance, produced a record equalling score of 67, whilst Sandy Lyle, a US Masters' Champion, was one of 30 players who failed to break 80. Nick Faldo, who had won the event in three of the previous four years, could only manage a 73. On the second day Bernard Langer challenged Torrance and they shared the half-way lead. Tony Jacklin successfully banished his putting blues using an old hickory-shafted putter for a 69. Torrance and Langer were still in the lead at the end of the third round. In the final round a tussle between Langer and Jacklin, both Ryder Cup captains, ensued with a critical three shot swing on the 16th green. Langer's drive went through the rear right of this long, two tier, hog's back green, and he took four putts to get down to Jacklin's birdie two. Statistics show that the 16th hole was the toughest on the course (Fig.90). After 72 holes, Langer and Jacklin were tied and 37-year-old Jacklin won the first play-off hole, the 15th, to gain his first major tournament victory in this country since 1973 and a prize of £13,300. Willie Whitelaw, Margaret Thatcher's Deputy Prime Minister and Captain of the R&A in 1969, presented the trophy.

The tournament was watched by an aggregate of over 21,000 paying spectators, including some 8,500 on the final day, breaking all attendance records for the event (Fig.91). The field of 450 entrants was a record for the PGA European Tour, and it included top players. Television coverage, amounting to over 15 hours, exceeded that for any tournament other than the Open Championship. Despite this apparent success this was to be the last occasion when Hillside hosted a major professional tournament. The clubs that had done so much to help to nurture the development of professional tournament golf would see the European Tour move events to the new generation of commercially provided venues, frequently abroad. By 2010, the Tour scheduled only one tournament in England and that on a commercially owned course.

If clubs wanted professional competitions to be played on their courses, they normally had to settle for staging lower status events involving lesser-known players. Unlike the European Tour these events attract limited media coverage.

A hastily arranged **PGA International Cup** between teams of club professionals representing the United States and Great Britain and Ireland (a mini Ryder Cup) was played at Hillside in 1975. Although the home team was managed by Ryder Cup veteran Christie O'Connor and included former Open

Fig.90 *Sun Alliance PGA Championship 1982. Tony Jacklin putting on the 16th green.*

Fig.91 *Sun Alliance PGA Championship 1982. This event attracted a record numbers of spectators.*

Fig.92 *PGA International Team Cup 1975. The flag raising ceremony.*

Champion Max Faulkner the match attracted little attention and was won comfortably by the United States team (Fig.92).

In 1989 the **PGA Assistants' Championship** for the Peugeot Cup was played at Hillside and won by Colin Brooks. This was a competition with an outstanding pedigree, in terms of the names of former winners. But part of the revolution in tournament golf was the fact that amateurs no longer had to face the protectionist hurdle of the Professional Golf Association's rigidly enforced qualification regulations that had included a five-year waiting period. Consequently top tournament golfers seldom emerge from amongst the ranks of contemporary assistants. 1990 saw the **Peugeot Cup** competition return to Hillside for the diamond jubilee of this PGA event. One of the four rounds had to be abandoned because of the high winds that resulted in the ball moving on the exposed 13th green. The winner Tony Ashton equalled the course record of 66 for his first round, but it did not stand as it was the medal rather than the championship course that was being played.

There was another PGA event in 1990 – the **Golf Plus Four Ball Championship**. Although there was a prize fund of £24,000, the nature of the field was again characterised by the obscurity of the winners. There was one familiar name on the list, Bernard Hunt, a former Ryder Cup player and captain. This veteran, comfortably past his 60th birthday, tied for the lead in the first round.

Hillside did host a major tournament in 2003 but it was a senior event being staged as part of the Merseyside Festival of Golf - the **Merseyside English Seniors' Open Championship**. Sponsorship and TV rights had enabled the European Seniors Tour to develop a lucrative circuit; at Hillside the prize was £22,500. Nevertheless some of the Senior Tour events were still played on club courses. After qualification there was a field of 83 competing and there was no further 'cut' during the three-day tournament. Before the start Carl Mason, the leader of the Seniors' Tour Order of Merit, was quoted as saying: 'Hillside is a marvellous course, I love it. It has to be one of the most under rated in the whole British Isles.' (Fig.93) He went on to win the first prize and in doing so again secured top spot in the annual Order of Merit. The prize for the Super Senior (over 60-years-of-age) went to Tommy Horton, one of professional golf's gentlemen, who had won the Piccadilly Medal Match Play tournament at Hillside over 30 years earlier, and was to enjoy over 20 victories on the Senior Tour.

British ladies were slow to follow their American counterparts in establishing a ladies' professional golf circuit. But attitudes were changing and it was not to be long before Laura Davies and her contemporaries were leading the charge into the new era of open competitions. Ladies' open golf tournaments did not have the marketing clout of the men's game. Consequently the ladies were happy to use club courses for their events. **The Ladies' United Kingdom Open Championship**

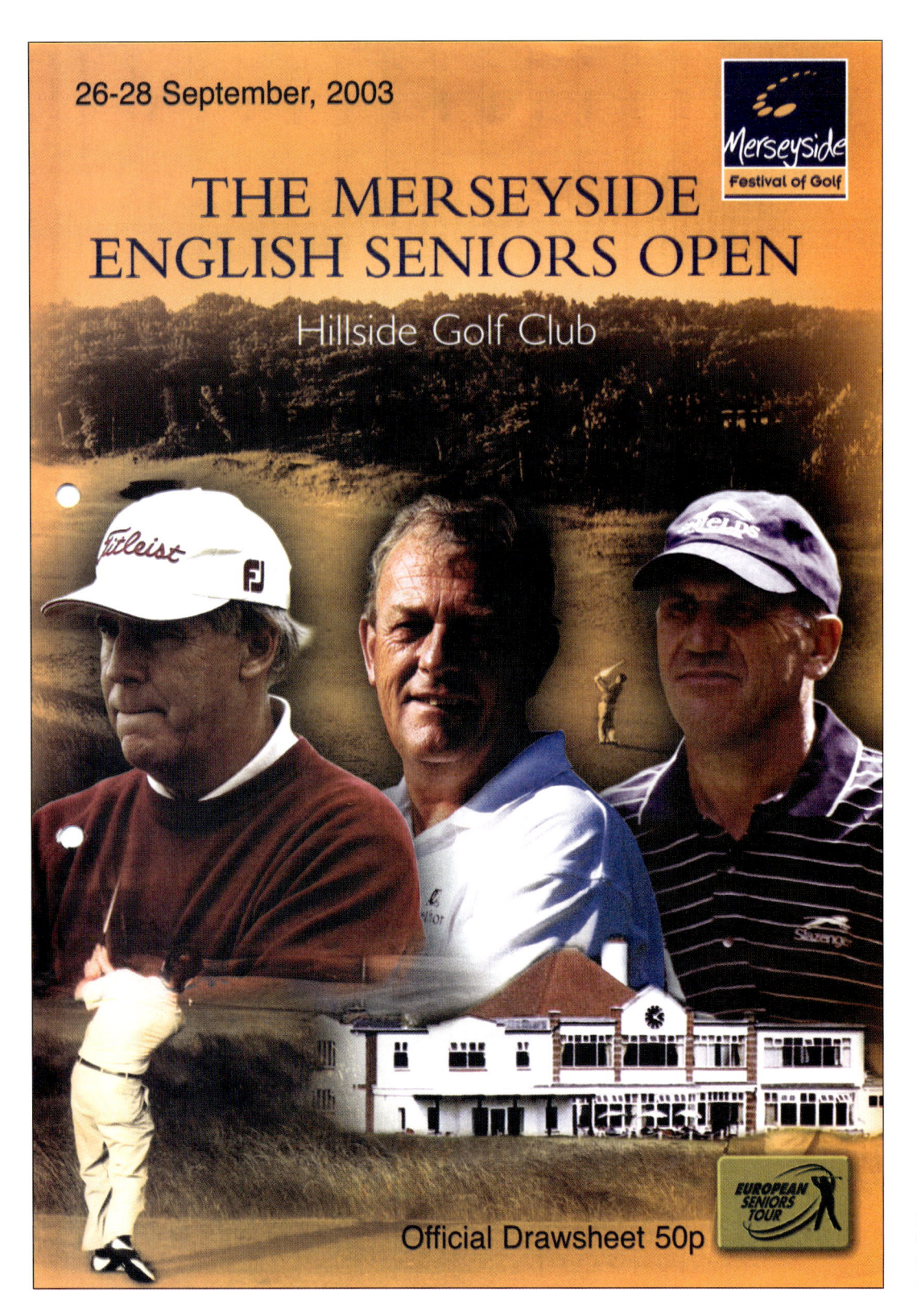

Fig.93 *The Merseyside English Seniors' Open Championship 2003. Carl Mason is the middle of the three golfers featured on this programme cover.*

(the Weetabix) was played at Royal Birkdale in 2005 and Hillside was used as the sole qualifying course. There was a record 315 entries, of which 140 were exempt from qualification, leaving ten spots for qualifiers from Hillside. The field at Royal Birkdale included World number one Annika Sorenstam and 15-year-old American amateur sensation Michelle Wie. The Championship (now the Ricoh) returned to Royal Birkdale in 2010 and Hillside was again the qualifying course (Fig.94). This tournament is the only women's major to be played outside the United States. The leading qualifier was Lynette Brooky and her score of 67 is believed to be the lowest recorded by a lady professional at Hillside.

The Open
Championship Qualifying

The Open Championship and its qualification process are outside the control of the European Tour and the PGA. In 1920, long before the Open had become an international phenomenon, the committee of participating clubs, who had formerly run it, passed on the responsibility to the R&A. Consequently the allocation of venues for the Open is still a matter for the R&A, as is the selection of qualifying courses. The Open is played annually on one of a limited number of seaside links courses, which include Royal Birkdale and Royal Lytham. Hillside has served as a qualifying course for both. When a club is nominated as one of the qualifying courses it receives a facility fee from the R&A whose agronomist is then involved in the preparation of the course. When the Open is at Royal Birkdale, Hillside also receives a fee for the use of the practice ground for a car park and further income is generated by using the clubhouse for corporate hospitality.

When the Open returned to Royal Birkdale in **1971**, the final qualifying courses were Hillside, Hesketh and S&A. At Hillside tournament tees stretched the course to 7,064 yards, Stuart Brown set a new professional record of 67, and Peter Alliss was one of the 29 qualifiers. It was an Open of charismatic personalities. Extrovert Supermex, Lee Trevino, was a popular winner, but the runner-up, Mr 'Lu', the little known Formosan, ever-smiling, pork-pie-hat-raising outsider, also captivated the crowds.

Hillside was again used for qualifying in **1976** when Mark James, later to be the Ryder Cup captain, set a record of 68 for a revised course. The number of qualifying spots allocated to Hillside had been reduced to 18, and American Johnny Miller was the champion at Royal Birkdale.

There were 19 qualifiers from Hillside when the Open returned

Fig.94 *Ricoh Women's British Open Championship – Final Qualifying 2010. Lynette Brooky, the leading qualifier.*

to Royal Birkdale in **1983**. They included Simon Hobday from South Africa and Australian Peter Senior. Ryder Cup player Howard Clark, now a TV commentator, had the benefit of a pre-tournament reconnaissance of the course with Hillside's Gordon Rimmer, and qualified in second place. The scores indicated that Hillside was the most challenging of the four qualifying courses and the *Southport Visiter* golf correspondent suggested that Hillside was the course '...that really sorted them out.' Tom Watson followed Peter Thomson's feat in winning his fifth Open at Royal Birkdale.

Hillside was a qualifying course once more in 1991. As so often was the case, those who tied for the remaining places had to play off. Those with a total of 148 for the two qualifying rounds were involved. Two of the three available slots were quickly taken but it took another 16 holes to decide the final qualifier. The play-off started on the Monday night and was completed on the Tuesday morning when Jimmy Heggarty was eliminated but became first reserve for the championship. This was not, however, the end of the drama. He became a last minute qualifier when Ronan Rafferty withdrew and only just made his starting time. Ian Baker-Finch, a personable young Australian, had a winning total of 272, comfortably the lowest score ever achieved in an Open Championship at Royal Birkdale.

There were only 13 qualifying spots at Hillside when the championship returned to Royal Birkdale in **1998** (Fig.95). The weather was harsh and Australian Roger Pampling, the first day leader, later described Hillside as the hardest course he had ever played. The qualifiers included New Zealander Michael Campbell and the Spaniard Miguel Angel Jimenez. The runner-up at Hillside was a young English amateur Justin Rose. Barely 17-years-old, Justin then enjoyed three extraordinary days at Birkdale including a score of 66, in the second round played in brutal conditions, to equal the record low score by an amateur in the Open. He went on to threaten the leaders on the final day. When he holed his pitch for a three on the 18th green he raised possibly the loudest cheer of the day and finished with the amateur silver medal and a share of fourth place, the best result for an amateur in almost 50 years and he immediately turned professional. Mark O'Meara was champion after winning the first ever play-off at Royal Birkdale.

Hillside's status as a championship course was confirmed when the Open was held at Royal Lytham in **2001** and Hillside was selected as one of the four qualifying courses for a championship that was being played on the northern side of the Ribble. Mark James, who had set a course record 25 years earlier, was amongst the qualifiers from Hillside. The German Alex Cejka and Australian Stephen Leaney jointly set a new course record of 65. Amongst the competitors was Australian Wayne Riley, who became an enthusiastic advocate of the course's quality.

The success of the Open, in terms of generating gate revenue and television fees was reflected in the amount of prize money distributed. There had also been a massive growth in the number of players seeking the opportunity to qualify. The R&A had no wish to run an invitation event. In principle the Open Championship is open to the entire world. By the year 2000, the number seeking to qualify had soared to 2,480, whilst the number of competitors who would play in the championship proper was limited to 156. In an attempt to encourage international participation and save foreign golfers the expense of wasted journeys to attempt qualification, the R&A decided to introduce earlier final qualifying competitions in Africa, Asia, Australia, Europe, the United States and in Britain. This 2004 amendment led to the number of qualifying spots left for final local qualifying being much reduced. In 1998 there were 120 competitors seeking to qualify at Hillside and there were 13 spots available, whilst in 2008 this was reduced to four. Big name players, particularly from overseas, now seldom appear at this stage. Final local qualification has become an event for lower-ranked tournament professionals, club professionals and amateurs who have fought their way through the regional pre-qualifiers.

The list for final local qualifying at Hillside in **2008** confirmed the changed nature of the qualifying system. Some three weeks before the Open, the European qualifying competition was played at Sunningdale for 18 spots. The competitors contesting these places included three members of the last Ryder Cup team.

The final local qualifying was played on three courses on the Monday and Tuesday of the week before the Open, rather than on the traditional weekend immediately prior to the Open. In 1998 the Hillside list had featured a high proportion of professional players with international reputations. In 2008, 19 of the 96 competitors at Hillside were amateurs and the list included few familiar names. Two of the four qualifiers at Hillside were amateurs. At Royal Birkdale, the players faced gale-force winds and Padraig Harrington joined the elite group of back-to-back Open Champions. Chris Wood, one of the amateurs who qualified at Hillside, was to go on to win the silver medal and more remarkably to finish in fifth place overall. Like the previous year's winner of the medal he immediately turned professional. Extraordinarily, this rookie professional went on to tie for third place in the following year's Open.

Amateur Golf

The changes in the professional game have influenced the amateur game. Few of the top amateur golfers retain this status long enough to play in a second Walker Cup fixture. All of the 2009 team were first-time rookies. The Amateur Championship competitors are getting younger, so much so that the R&A, that had earlier introduced a Youth

Fig.95 *The 127th Open Championship Qualifying 1998.*

Championship to fill the gap between the Boys Championship and the Amateur Championship, removed it in 1995, because of the degree of overlap that was occurring. The oversight of amateur tournaments is split between the R&A and the English Golf Union (EGU). Amateur championship golf has become a stepping stone for precocious youth to move into the professional tournament ranks. Gone is the PGA's requirement that former amateurs should serve an apprenticeship or a qualifying period. The Mid-Amateur Championship replaced the Youth Championship for players, with a minimum age qualification of 35. These are players who were being squeezed out of the Amateur Championship by successive cohorts of young players.

Since the course reconstruction in the 1960s, the Club has repeatedly been invited to host national and international amateur events. Increasingly it is amateur competitions that showcase top players at Hillside. Some of the youngsters involved go on to establish international professional reputations.

In 1971, the EGU's **English Amateur Open Stroke Play Championship** (the Brabazon) was played at Hillside for the first time. Ian Mosey, a former British boys and youth international who later turned professional, set a new amateur record of 69 on the altered course, but Michael Bonallack, five times winner of the Amateur Championship and the leading British amateur golfer of his generation, who was to become a distinguished administrator and secretary of the R&A, was the champion (Fig.96). Hillside members Gordon Rimmer, Steve Rooke and Michael Pearson took part, with Michael getting through to the final day.

The EGU's **Home International Championship**, for the Raymond Trophy, was played at Hillside in 1977 (Fig.97). England won the Championship after three tight matches, scraping home with a one game margin in the deciding match against Scotland. Ironically future Open and US Masters' champion Sandy Lyle, a Scot, played for England.

The **Amateur Championship**, the Blue Ribbon event of British

Fig.96 English Open Amateur Stroke Play 1971.
Captain John Giddens presents the Brabazon Trophy to Michael Bonallack.

amateur golf, was awarded by the R&A to Hillside in 1979 and produced two American finalists, fresh from their participation in the United States' victorious Walker Cup team at Muirfield. The winner was 34-year-old Jay Sigel (Fig.98). Whilst at college he had ambitions to progress to the professional tour, but his dream was shattered by a domestic accident which left him needing 76 stitches in a hand wound. Unable to play golf he concentrated on building an insurance business, before later later combining his work with a career in amateur golf, winning the US Amateur Championship on two occasions and played in nine consecutive Walker Cup matches. He belatedly achieved his college ambition when he joined the US PGA Seniors' Tour in 1995 and within 10 years amassed over seven million dollars. Scott Hoch was the runner-up and

Fig.97 *EGU Home International Championship 1977.*

Fig.98 *Amateur Championship 1979.*
Jay Sigel driving from the 10th tee in the final.

turned professional after the championship. Hillside was strongly represented by Mike Walls, Rob Godley, Fred Wilson and Paul Buckels.

Two years later the **English Amateur Open Stroke Play Championship** (the Brabazon) returned to Hillside. Louis Stanley wrote that: 'Promising youngsters not only threaten major players with established reputations but have won several major events.' He cited the success of Ronan Rafferty as a 17-year-old. The title went to another youngster, Paul Way, and the runner-up was Richard Boxall. All three of these players later distinguished themselves in the professional game. Peter McEvoy, who had an outstanding and long career as a player and administrator in the amateur game, shared third spot with Hillside's Rob Godley. Despite soggy, windy conditions Paul Way took Rob Godley's amateur course record with a round of 67. Mike Walls also competed.

Hillside's run of being invited to stage leading amateur competitions continued and in 1986 the **English Men's Amateur Championship** came to the Club. The weather was mixed but spectators turned out in good numbers. Jonathan Langmead, aged 18, was the youngest winner since Nick Faldo and was selected to play for England in the Home International Championship. There were no Hillside players involved in the final stages.

The format of the Amateur Championship had changed in 1983. There were to be two rounds of stroke play after which 64 players would go forward to contest the match play rounds. One of the qualifying rounds was to be played on the course used for the match play rounds and a second course was nominated for the other 18 holes. This change allowed the number of entrants to be increased from 256 to 288 and ensured that they all played at least two competitive rounds, with one being on the primary course. When the **Amateur Championship** returned to Royal Birkdale to mark its centenary year in 1989, it was paired with Hillside. In John Beherend's history of the championship he wrote that: '...low scores at Hillside are just as hard to come by as Birkdale.' Ernie Els, qualified with a total of 149, but his car was broken into and his clubs stolen and, playing with borrowed clubs, he made an early departure from the knockout stage.

In 1991 Hillside hosted the first **European Amateur Open Championship** to be played outside continental Europe. There were so many entries that a qualifying competition had to be held for those with handicaps of scratch and one. The winner was Jim Payne, who in the same year won the amateur silver medal in the Open Championship and the British Youth Championship (Fig.99). He turned professional and was the Rookie of the Year, won two tournaments including the Italian Open, and qualified for the Open Championship three times. Nevertheless he quit the tour to take the post of professional at S&A.

Fig.99 *European Amateur Open Championship 1991. Jim Payne playing out of a bunker on the 18th hole.*

1995 saw the **English Amateur Open Stroke Play Championship** (The Brabazon) played yet again at Hillside. The event produced joint champions Colin Edwards, who equalled the amateur course record of 67, and Mark Foster,

Fig.100 *British Mid-Amateur Championship 1996. Gary Wolstenholme receives the trophy from Captain Derek Anderson.*

Fig.101 *Home International Championship 2009. Tommy Fleetwood driving from the 17th tee.*

the current English Amateur Champion who went on to a successful professional career. Five Hillside players took part: Paul Buckels, Rob Godley, Greg Helsby, Phil Kenyon and Stuart Taylor. Rob got through to the final day and tied for 12th place.

The **British Mid-Amateur Championship**, which had been devised for older, long-term amateurs, was held at Hillside in 1996. Walker Cup player Gary Wolstenholme, who won the trophy on two other occasions, was champion (Fig.100).

The **European Men's Team Championship** was played at Hillside in 2005. This was only the second time that this championship was played in England; it had previously been held on the Royal St George links 40 years earlier. England beat the German team in the final, the first English success for 14 years. The six-man team included Oliver Fisher, Gary Lockerbie and Gary Wolstenholme. Other notable competitors were Northern Ireland's Rory McIlroy and Germany's Martin Kaymer.

A feature of the new generation of players in the teams contesting the **Home International Championship** at Hillside in 2009 was their youth. Wales had the youngest player, Rhys Pugh at only 15 years. England, with seven Walker Cup players, all rookies, started as favourites to win. Scotland arrived as European and world champions, and Ireland as reigning champions, but England emerged as champions. Figuring strongly for England was local boy Tommy Fleetwood (Fig.101). A fortnight later this 18-year-old, with a handicap of plus five, went on to play in the Walker Cup team in the United States. When he joined the professional ranks in 2010 he was the highest ranked European in world amateur golf and the English Amateur Champion.

The Ladies' County Finals returned to Hillside in 1968 and once again Surrey won the championship. Hillside hosted the **Ladies' British Amateur Open Championship** for the first time in 1977. A strong field of 101 players included a number of leading international players, and Angela Uzielli, the wife of the Millennium Year Captain of the R&A, was the champion (Fig.102). The **Ladies' Home International Championship** was also played at Hillside in 1977.

Hillside has hosted Britain's principal competition for boys - the **Boys' Championship** – on two occasions. The R&A took over the organisation of this 84-year-old competition in 1948. Past champions have included James Bruen, Jose Maria Olazabal, Sergio Garcia, Howard Clark, and David Howell.

Shortly after the completion of the course reconstruction, the Boys' Championship was transferred to Hillside in 1970 from the designated course, Seaton Carew, because of the disturbance to that course by the construction of a power station. Burnley boy Ian Gradwell won the title, having previously won the Lancashire Boys' Championship for a record three years. He was the most exciting young player of his generation and turned professional but enjoyed only modest success as a tournament player before settling for a career as a club professional. The tournament returned to Hillside in 2000, when Denis Inglis was champion and over a fifth of the 256 competitors were from overseas (Fig.103). The entrants included England's Nick Dougherty and Gary Lockerbie, the Bourdy brothers from France, Spaniards Alejandrio Canizares and Pablo Lazzarabal, and Italy's Francesco Molinari. Home interest was further fuelled by the inclusion of Hillside member Andrew Sumner. Danny Belch who was subsequently to join the Club also took part. In 2006 the Club hosted the international match between English Schools and Scottish Schools.

The **Lancashire Union of Golf Clubs** has regularly played its inter-county games at Hillside. Hillside also hosted the Lancashire Union's Championship in 1983 and 2003. In 1983, Hillside member Mike Walls was able to provide the Club with a home winner (Fig.104); whilst in 2003 Hillside won the team championship. This was the first time that this championship was played under a stroke play format.

Hillside was also a venue of choice for the **Lancashire Ladies' County Golf Association**. In 1970, the Club hosted the ladies' Northern Division Inter-County Championship, in which Hillside member 16-year-old Carline Eckersley played for Lancashire.

The Club launched its own amateur open scratch tournament for The **Pines Trophy** in 1975. It became part of the regional circuit of category one open events and is now one of the Mitsushiba Northern Order of Merit events that are played around the north west on most summer Sundays. The list of winners of the Pines Trophy is a who's who of regional amateur golf and includes a number of players who have gone on to professional careers, most notably player Lee Westwood, who won as a 17-year-old from the Worksop Club in 1990 and became world number one in 2010 (Fig.105), Paul Eales, Steve Webster and local boy Lee Slattery. Hillside winners have been Mike Walls, on two occasions, and Mark Prue.

Fig.102 *Ladies' British Amateur Open Championship 1977. Angela Uzielli receives her trophy from the Captain, John McAlister.*

Fig.103 *The Boys' Amateur Championship 2000.*

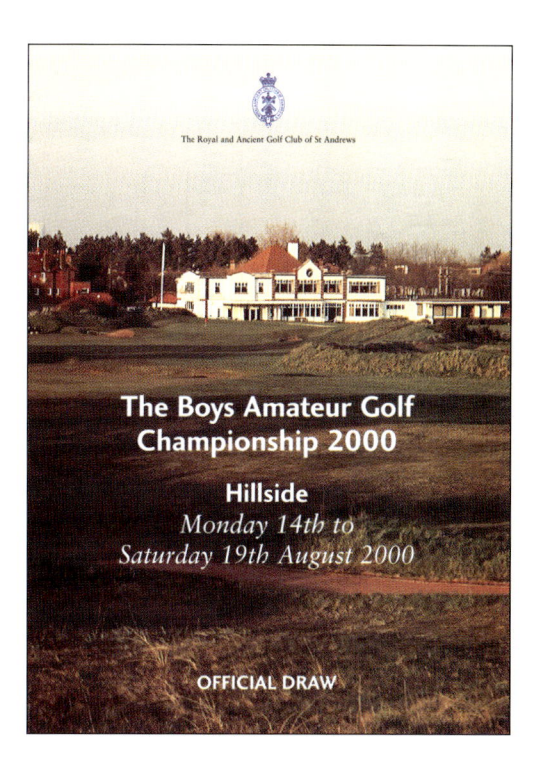

Fig.104 *Lancashire Union of Golf Clubs Championship 1983. Mike Walls celebrating his win with Captain, Bill Backhouse.*

Fig.105 *Hillside Pines Trophy 1990. A youthful Lee Westward receiving the trophy from Captain George Owen.*

Chapter Nine
Club Professionals, Champions and Championships
1967 - 2010

The Club Professionals
John Hewitt 1972-1982

As a boy John caddied at the Northcliffe course in Shipley, near Bradford and regularly 'sneaked' on to the course to play the holes out of sight from the clubhouse. In 1948, at the age of 16, he successfully applied for a vacancy, which had been advertised for the job of third assistant professional to Jim Wade at Bradford Golf Club. Wade was to ensure that John learned his place and served his apprenticeship in the traditional manner. For two years he was not allowed to play with members, to teach, or to join the PGA. He worked on clubs in the workshop until noon each day and was then allowed to practise until 2pm. The afternoon was spent back at the bench until 4.30pm in winter and 7pm in summer after which he was allowed to practise or to play. His wage was 21s 6d (£1.07) a week. He continued as a third assistant for two years prior to being called-up for National Service. When he was demobilised two years later he rejoined Wade as first assistant.

Fig.106 *John Hewitt. Serious swinging in the 1970s.*

In 1953 Wade was appointed as the professional at the old Moor Allerton course, near Leeds, and John went with him as a teaching/playing assistant and in 1955 he became the professional at Wilpshire Golf Club, near Blackburn. In 1959 the club wanted to combine this role with that of greenkeeper, thus creating a post that did not appeal to John and he took the post of professional at Renishaw Park (Sheffield). John still aspired to succeed playing in professional tournaments. The four round regional tournaments he played in normally yielded between £25 and £35, for players who qualified for the final two rounds, which were played on a Friday. John achieved modest success and was the Sheffield Professional Champion in 1960, and reached the quarterfinals of the British Match Play Championship in 1963. It was at Renishaw that he met his wife Janet, now a long-standing member of Hillside.

In 1965 John moved from Sheffield to Sweden as professional at the Linkoping course, which is owned by the Saab Aircraft Company. He was in at the start of the golf revolution that occurred in Sweden. As chief instructor of the course for assistant professionals John played a significant part in the country's spectacular rise in the world of golf. He also led the money earners on the Scandinavian professional circuit in 1966. Concern about his children's education caused him to return to this country in 1972.

Burton had retired at Hillside and Hewitt was appointed to fill the vacancy. He had developed as a teaching professional and coach, and attracted pupils from other clubs. In the late 1970s the English Golf Union appointed him as its North-West Regional Golf Coach. This was a post that brought him into contact with the region's leading young players.

Although achieving a growing reputation as a teacher, John still found time and the motivation to play in some tournaments (Fig.106). The quality of his game is evident from his record in the Open Championship. On three occasions he qualified for the championship proper and in 1974, at Royal Lytham, at a time when the field was cut twice, after the second and the third rounds, he qualified for the final day. In 1976, at West Lancashire, he had to withdraw from the final qualifying suffering from severe sunstroke. He continued the Hillside's professional involvement with the Liverpool Alliance and served as its captain for two years. Playing with Gordon Rimmer he reached the semi-finals of the Spalding Cup in 1977. In the same year he also won the Guy Taylor Trophy in the Liverpool and District Meeting. Nevertheless it is a teacher that many will remember John.

Fig.107 *Brian Seddon. Behind the counter in his shop 1991.*

Brian Seddon (1982-)

Enthused by golf lessons he received as a boy, Brian Seddon decided that he wanted to become a professional golfer, and his teacher, Jimmy Hume the Formby professional, encouraged him in this ambition. Brian had no record in amateur representative golf, but when he left school Hume took him on as an assistant. This was the traditional way of entering the profession. He served his apprenticeship and passed the PGA examination which qualified him to become a club professional. His first move was along the 'Line' to gain further experience by joining Brian Janes at West Lancashire, as a teaching professional.

He was appointed professional at Alderley Edge Golf Club in 1974. His role as professional was combined with that of greenkeeper of this nine-hole course. He moved to Heaton Moor, a club with an 18-hole course, in 1978, but returned to Merseyside a year later, when he was appointed to the West Derby Golf Club.

Brian arrived at Hillside in 1982. His career has not featured much participation in tournament golf although members who have played with him testify as to the quality of his game. He has had four holes-in-one and needs only the 4th to bag the lot at Hillside. Brian came near to scoring an albatross on the par five 3rd hole at Royal Liverpool, when playing with Captain Gerry Brunskill in a Volvo PGA competition. His long second shot struck the flagstick and came to rest alongside the hole for an eagle. The link between the Hillside professional's shop and the Liverpool Alliance did not loom as large as had been the case in previous years; it seems that some of the Alliance's earlier function of providing local opportunities for professionals to conveniently compete with their fellows had been superseded by the emergence of a number of minor professional tours.

Brian does, however, take his teaching role seriously and is well regarded by his pupils. When interviewed by a journalist for an article in Golf World in 1991, he stated that: 'It's rewarding to see people improve, to see a member win a club competition after having a lesson with you.' An innovative teacher, he embraced new technology in his teaching strategies. He also enjoys his shop having recognised the realities of competitive trading, with so many other outlets chasing golfers' business. Brian attempted to offer members and visitors a level of personal professional service with his sales that was not available in the golf superstores or on the internet (Fig.107). Brian's eye for business was revealed when he was involved in a lavishly illustrated article on golf fashions for ladies, which appeared in a local newspaper during the week of the Open Championship at Royal Birkdale in 1983, and was the sole listed local stockist of the featured lines. Similarly in the previous year he inserted adverts in the Southport Visiter when the Sun-Alliance PGA tournament was played at Hillside.

Regular contact with members is maintained in collecting fees for competitions. A staunch supporter of the captain, Brian regularly partners him in Sunday morning challenge matches with members. In his report to the AGM, one captain commented on Brian's unfailing good humour in these games. If John Burton was the golf professionals' professional, Brian Seddon probably qualifies for the description of a members' professional.

Brian has not employed an assistant for some time but is supported by his brother, Peter, the shop manager, and Dave Wheeler, a PGA qualified professional, who also assists in the shop and undertakes a regular teaching commitment in Brian's academy. After 29 years service, Brian is now looking forward to moving to his new shop.

Hillside's Champions

With a links course that could stand comparison with the best, Hillside assembled a strong scratch team that challenged for honours. The quality of the course, the appointment of a professional who was to become the EGU's North-West Regional Coach, and the presence of other achieving golfers, meant that the Club was able to attract top-class recruits

Fig.108 *Gordon Rimmer. On the right, playing in the Brabazon at Hillside in 1971.*

rather than to continue to lose promising golfers to other clubs. The Club also benefited from the encouragement that had been given to its youngsters, which was producing potential players for the scratch team. The result was an increase in the number of Hillside members gaining representative honours.

Gordon Rimmer, an English international rugby player and a British and Irish Lion, had already begun to make an impact on Hillside golf before the reconstructed course was opened. Following in the footsteps of his father and his uncle, he joined the Club in 1946, after aircrew service with the RAF. For a number of years commitment to rugby limited his opportunity to play golf. Nevertheless this talented all-round sportsman, who also excelled at water polo and cricket, continued to reduce his handicap, which stood at 15 in 1952. By 1957 he achieved his first major win, the Hodkinson Scratch Trophy and, after becoming a scratch golfer, he was selected to play for Lancashire in 1965. He was only the second Hillside member to achieve this honour but was to lose his only game for the county. He played in the qualifying round of the Brabazon, when it was held at Hillside in 1971 (Fig.108). A competitive golfer, Gordon was to have nine major wins within the Club during a career spanning more than 50 years. He also captained the scratch team.

After a period as a partner in a local sports' outfitting business, Gordon was to shape his working life to complement his commitment to the game. He was variously a golf equipment manufacturer's representative, an agent for golf equipment, a starter for the PGA, and a custodian of a mobile advertising display at professional tournaments.

Gordon's contribution to the Club was not confined to the course. He was an active committee man with particular concern for Hillside's youngsters. Gordon held strong views on all things concerning golf. On the course he set himself high standards in relation to punctuality, speed of play and etiquette and expected the same from others, regardless of their status or reputation. In the millennium year he was made a Life Member, an honour he shared with David Marsh, Southport's most distinguished contemporary golfer.

Following a glittering junior career, Hillside youngster **Steve Rooke** was runner-up in the Lancashire Championship and joint second in the English Amateur Championship in 1970. Between 1970 and 1974 he represented Lancashire 17 times, winning six matches, halving one and losing ten. Steve was a member of both Hillside and S&A and although the Lancashire Golf Union Handbook lists him as an S&A player, Steve told Phil Irlam that: 'I always saw myself as a member of Hillside, where I spent more of my time.' He played for the scratch team and his name appears on the Club's honours boards four times, compared to a single appearance at S&A. He did, however, play under the banner of S&A in county events thus allowing him to be included in S&A's powerful and successful team in the Lancashire Team Championship. Hillside was not to have a team strong enough to consistently contend in this event until the mid-1980s.

Steve's brief amateur career came to an end in 1974 when he became an assistant to Hillside professional John Hewitt. He spurned a university place in order to take this post and achieved some tournament success, including a good run in the Open at Carnoustie, before settling as a successful club professional at Windermere (Fig.109).

Fig.109 *Steve Rooke. Professional at Windermere Golf Club.*

Mike Pearson, another former junior member, also figured in the scratch team. When the Brabazon Tournament was played at Hillside in 1971, he distinguished himself by qualifying for the last day. With his handicap down to one, he won the 36 holes Liverpool and District Open Championship, which was played at Royal Liverpool, in 1973. It was an event open to both amateurs and professionals, in which an amateur victory was rare. Mike produced the day's lowest score, a 72 for his afternoon round. In the same year he was a joint leader in the first of the two qualifying rounds (The Rayner Batty Trophy) for the Lancashire Amateur Championship. He was selected to play for Lancashire against Cumberland and Westmorland, halving his only game. Within the Club he won the Aggregate Trophy, the Hodkinson Scratch Trophy, and the Ex-Captain's Four Ball Cup.

Hillside's most successful player to date is **Mike Walls**, who joined the Club as a 25-year-old in 1978, after a productive early golfing career in Cumbria. He had played for England Boys and over 60 times for Cumbria; he won the Cumbria County Championship four times, the county match play title twice and the prestigious County Champions' Golf Tournament in 1977. Sundry other titles won included Royal Birkdale's Goblet.

A career move brought this bank employee into the Southport district and his decision to join Hillside was a consequence of the presence of John Hewitt, the North-West Regional Coach, with whom he had previously worked. The newcomer rapidly made his mark and in 1979 he won the Lancashire Championship at his initial attempt thus becoming the first Hillside member to hold the title. He was to be champion a second time in 1983, when the championship was played at Hillside and was runner-up three years later. Between 1979 and 1987 he played in 65 matches for Lancashire, winning 43, halving eight and losing on only 14 occasions. His percentage of victories is the highest ever achieved by a Lancashire player.

Selection for the England team to play in the Home International Championship came in 1980, making him the Club's first full amateur international. He was again selected in 1981 and 1985, and finished with a record of 15 matches won, none halved and six lost.

Playing on the regional category one open scratch circuit, he gained a number of titles; victories in Hillside's Pines Trophy in 1983 and 1984 must have been particularly pleasing. Arguably his greatest achievement was to win the Lytham Trophy in 1985 (Fig.110). This prestigious event attracts leading golfers from the four home unions and is always over-subscribed. Perhaps his most memorable game, however, was in the Amateur Championship at Formby in 1984. Here he encountered future two-time US Masters' Champion Spain's Jose Maria Olazabal. Mike was to lose a fiercely contested game on the 18th.

Fig.110 *Mike Walls. The Lytham Trophy 1985*

For players of Mike's status, who are committed to so much representative golf, their club record can appear to be modest. Despite this he did win five of Hillside's major competitions.

After initially moving to North Wales, where he continued to collect representative golf honours playing for Flintshire and North Wales, Mike was able to make a second career within golf by becoming a club secretary. His first appointment at Taunton and Pickeridge also enabled him to extend his representative career by playing for Somerset for six years. During this period he qualified to play in what he described as a memorable tournament in Sun City, South Africa. In 2007, he returned to Lancashire to become secretary of Clitheroe Golf Club and is now looking forward to the possibility of a return to representative golf with Lancashire Seniors.

Rob Godley is an example of home-grown talent, having been an outstanding junior golfer at Hillside. He won The Custom and Excise Championship in Leeds in 1980, and further signalled his strength in outside events in the following year when he finished in joint third place in the English Open Amateur Stroke Play Championship, which was played at Hillside.

This result was sufficient to earn him selection for the Lancashire County team Subsequently he played 25 times for Lancashire, winning 11 matches, halving five and losing nine. His best individual success in the county championship was as runner-up in 1994.

1985 brought victory in the Royal Birkdale Goblet. Other local scratch open event successes were in Hesketh's Henriques Trophy, West Lancashire's Crosby Challenge Plate, the Penwortham Bowl and the Southport & Ainsdale Bowl.

At the national level Rob won the Logan Trophy for the English Open Mid-Amateur Championship, for over 35-year-olds, at S&A in 1993 (Fig.111).

Within the Club he has been a prolific winner. His successes include seven victories in the Hodkinson Scratch Trophy, and six in the Captain's Prize, most recently in 2008. Included in his seven wins in the Ex-Captain's Four Ball Competition are two with his father, John Godley.

After a long career as a successful scratch team player, Rob now makes an additional contribution to the Club as a member of the Board of Directors.

Paul Williams initially played at Bootle Golf Club. He won the Lancashire Schoolboys' Championship in 1983 and joined Hillside in the following year. He played for Lancashire schoolboys' team and represented and captained the Liverpool University side in a team that won the English University Championships in each of his three undergraduate years. He was selected to play for British Universities against an American team at St Andrews and competed in the Boyd Quaich, the International Students' Championship, which was also played at St Andrews.

He played for Lancashire at colts' level and was Merseyside Colts' Champion in 1988. He twice came near to winning the Lancashire Championship, finishing second in 1988 and third

Fig.111 *Rob Godley. The Logan Mid-Amateur Championship Trophy 1993.*

Fig.112 *Phillip Kenyon. Working with Martin Kaymer at the Shell Houston Tournament 2009.*

in 1991. These achievements were sufficient to earn him a place on the county team in 1988 and he went on to win six, lose seven and halve two of his 15 matches. Within the Club his seven successes include winning the Hodkinson Scratch Trophy three times, his most recent win was in the Ex-Captain's Four Ball in 2007. Paul was still a scratch player competing in the Lancashire Championship in 2010.

Steve Ashcroft was another player who launched his career at Bootle Municipal Course, winning the Wilson Open title in 1986 and 1987, with scores of 65 and 64, which shattered the previous course record of 68. By 1988 he was a Hillside member playing in the scratch team and was selected for the Lancashire County Team, winning one and losing two of his three matches. Steve appears to have been the last Hillside player to be part of a Spalding Cup winning pair. Alliance competitions seldom attract the support of modern low handicap players. He was also the first Hillside player to win the Henriques Cup, Hesketh's open scratch competition. Playing at S&A he came close to qualifying for the 1991 Open Championship. After a score of 65 on the first day he missed qualifying by bogeying the last few holes of the second round. One par would have seen him through to play at Royal Birkdale. Oddly his brief spell at Hillside did not result in a win in any of the Club's major competitions.

Stuart Taylor learned his golf at Dean Wood, an inland course, and wanted to develop his game further by playing on a classic links course. He first played for Lancashire, who list him as a Hillside player, in 1995, winning three of his five games and losing two. Like Steve Ashcroft he played for the Club's scratch team but did not win any domestic competitions. In 1996 he became a professional but later reverted to amateur status as a member of Dean Wood, a decision he later reversed.

Phillip Kenyon was the son of Hillside members and came up through the Club's junior ranks. A student of sports science at John Moores University, Phil won the Bronze Medal for golf in the World Student Games, and captained both the English and Great Britain Universities golf teams. He made his county debut in 1993 and played in 15 games for Lancashire, winning seven, losing seven and halving one. In 1999 he and his partner Mark Prue won the Lancashire County Foursomes Championship. Within the Club he won the MacAvoy, Hodkinson and Buckels trophies. He also competed in national competitions, including the Brabazon at Hillside in 1995.

Phil turned professional in 2001 and played on the PGA Europro Tour and the European Challenge Tour. This professional playing experience in conjunction with his academic base - a first degree followed by a master's degree in applied psychology and sports science - gave him an ideal background to develop his career as a coach. For 18 years he had worked closely with Harold Swash, Hillside's 'Putting Doctor'. As Director of Instruction for Harold's Putting School of Excellence he now works as a performance coach to professional tournament players, particularly in relation to putting. He numbers several leading world class golfers, such as Henrik Stenson and Martin Kaymer, within his regular contracted clientele (Fig.112).

A number of other Hillside members have discovered what a competitive and expensive environment the foothills of professional golf can be. Mark Prue, a member of a Hillside family, played for Lancashire 'B' in 1998 and in the county side from a year later. He won eight of his 12 games and lost four. At Hillside he won the Founders' Trophy and the Hodkinson Scratch Trophy in 2000. He became one of the small band of home winners when he carried off Hillside's Pines Trophy in 1999, whilst other successes in open scratch competitions included winning the Southport and Ainsdale Bowl and the Fairhaven Pheasant. With his handicap at plus four he turned professional and played on the PGA Europro Tour. More recently he has withdrawn from professional competition and returned to Hillside as a playing member. His brother Steve also played for the scratch team, won the Collinge Trophy in 1989, and ventured into the professional game.

Danny Belch played for Lancashire between 2002 and 2006, winning 12 of his 23 games, losing nine and halving two. He had previously played for Lancashire Boys. Danny had taken up golf at the age of 13 and was a member at Pennington, a modest nine-hole municipal course, which is part of a country park near Leigh and played in the Boys' Championship at Hillside in 2000. As he developed his game he believed that wet and muddy winter conditions at Pennington were hindering his development and he joined Hillside. 'I wanted to improve my game', he told Liverpool Daily Post golf correspondent Harold Brough.

Danny was a welcome recruit for the scratch team. With a handicap of better than plus three, he played regularly in amateur tournaments enjoying top ten finishes in the Scottish and Irish amateur championships, played for the English 'B' Team and was a member of the 'A' Team squad. Danny turned professional in 2007, when he was 25-years-old. He plays on the Europro Tour, and has quickly discovered how difficult it is to meet the expense involved at this level.

Greg Helsby, a member of Grange Park, was the Lancashire Champion in 1993 and was a member of the county team winning seven of his 16 games and losing six with three halved. Later at Hillside he played for the scratch team and had a modest record in domestic competitions, winning two of the majors in 2002, but then enjoyed a golden year in 2008 when he won five of the Club's major trophies.

After winning the Lancashire Boys Championship in 2001, **Andrew Sumner,** a grandson of Harold Swash, was selected to play for the full Lancashire side and won two of his four matches. Still a Club member, the demands of a young family have restricted his playing opportunities in recent years.

In addition to those who gained representative honours there were a number of scratch team stalwarts who figured strongly on the Club's honours boards.

Harold Swash, an engineer, became a club manufacturer specialising in innovative putters. Designing putters made him analyse the fundamentals of the putting stroke and he became a successful teacher of this facet of the game. Harold was dubbed 'The Putting Doctor' and his clients included top tournament professionals as well as club members at all levels (Fig.113). He established the 'Harold Swash Putting School of Excellence' (HSPSE). A member of the early scratch team, he won all ten of the games that he played in the winning 1970 team. Later he was a member of the successful 1980s squad. In domestic competitions, he had eight successes including being a three times winner of the Hodkinson Scratch Trophy.

A win in the Captain's Prize in 1981 announced the arrival of **Mark Howard** as a golfing force at Hillside. He figured in scratch team successes and playing in the Pines Trophy in 1986 he beat SSS with a 73 and finished in fourth place. He was to become a regular visitor to the 'podium' and his win in the Founders' Trophy in 2007 was his 12th success.

Paul Buckels also established a distinguished record in Club competitions. His 14 victories between 1977 and 1995 include seven in the Hodkinson Scratch Trophy. For him 1978 was a golden year when he won four Club trophies.

Richie Blundell made a smooth transition from being an outstanding Hillside junior to becoming one of the Club's achieving scratch team players. In 2004 he won the Ex-Captain's Four Ball Trophy with his brother as partner, but it was a hat trick of victories in the Hodkinson Scratch Trophy that marked this scratch team player as one of the Club's leading performers. In 2009, he won the Captain's Prize and the Freddie Veale Trophy. With his handicap down to plus three, he became a regular in the county coaching squad and played for the 'B' team.

Fig.113 *Harold Swash (centre). The Putting Doctor ran a national putting championship at S&A. The runner-up was Hillside professional Brian Seddon (left), then attached to Alderley Edge Golf Club.*

His form translated into successes in external competitions and he won the Crosby Challenge Plate and was only one stroke behind the winner in the Hillside Pines Tournament. In 2010 he was runner-up in the Mitsubishi Northern Order of Merit. After a comfortable win in the Hulbert Trophy at Manchester Golf Club, Richie had a remarkable two round score of 130 to win the de Frece Trophy at Blackpool North Shore, by a margin of 11 shots (Fig.114).

Another group of promising scratch team golfers has come through from the junior ranks. **Ryan Gillespie** won the Hodkinson Scratch Trophy in 2009. In the same year, **Richard Kilshaw** was in the Lancashire coaching squad and **Mark O'Hara** is pushing hard behind.

Lancashire Seniors' Trophy

The increased opportunities for youngsters to play competitive golf are matched by similar developments for senior/veteran golfers. In 1974 **John McAlister**, the 1977 captain, was the Club's first winner of the Lancashire Seniors' Trophy. In the final of this 36 holes competition at Ormskirk, it took an inward half of 33, in the second round, to push him up the field and past the leaders. His consistency was demonstrated when he finished joint second in this event during his captaincy year and won for a second time in 1980. This time his final nine holes score of 31 enabled him to finish well clear of the field. Within the Club, John won the Captain's Prize at the age of 74 in 1992.

A Hillside member was again the Lancashire Seniors' Champion when the event was played at Hillside in 1986. **Tom Devaney**, a recently retired sea captain, who had previously enjoyed a low single figure handicap in Ireland, demonstrated that he was still a power off six. Tom's handicap slipped into double figures for the first time in 60 years in the year 2000.

The title returned to Hillside when **Harold Swash** won it in 1988 at Clitheroe. Harold was an experienced scratch team golfer and, although playing under the handicap of a heavy cold, his steadiness earned him a four stroke winning margin. Not surprisingly 'The Putting Doctor' attributed his success to '...two splendid putting rounds'. Harold also won the prestigious Marsh Harrier trophy in S&A's open senior tournament.

Other Outstanding Seniors

Other senior members with special achievements include: Chris Court, Hillside's one-armed bandit, who, competing with

Fig.114 *Richie Blundell 2010. Receiving the de Frece Trophy from the Captain of Blackpool North Shore Golf Club, Mr Brian Livesley.*

members blessed with their full complement of limbs, has won four of the Club's majors over a period of four decades; and John Simmons, who in 2009, at the age of 80, won the Collinge Trophy and became Hillside's oldest winner of 'a major'.

The Scratch Team

In addition to the individual Lancashire County Championship, there was a Lancashire Club Championship for a team of four with the lowest aggregate score, which had been contested since 1911. After World War II, the Championship was revived in 1948 and S&A was the champion club in 14 of the next 16 years. The emerging strength of the Hillside scratch team was reflected in the run of successes it enjoyed in this event in the 1980s, by which time

Fig.115 *Lancashire Team Champions, Hillside 1983.*
From the left: Rob Godley, Mark Howard, Mike Walls and Club Captain Roy Allan.

the championship was played as part of the two qualifying rounds and the team consisted of only three nominated players, each of whose 36 holes scores counted. Hillside's first win came in 1983 (Fig.115). Success was repeated in 1985, 1993, 1995 and 2003. With six wins, Hillside now holds second place to S&A in the number of championships won. The team has also been the runner-up on three occasions during this period, and in 1995 came third in the English National Club team finals.

Apart from the County Championship, which was completed in one weekend, low handicap golfers had limited opportunity to represent their club in team events. In 1963 a scratch team, selected by the Handicap Committee, played three eight-a-side matches against teams from other clubs. There was a demand for such fare and in 1968 a new competition, the Stephenson Newspapers' Winter League, was brought into being. It later became the *Southport Visiter* Winter Scratch League before coming under the auspices of a newly formed Southport and District Golf Association. Seven local clubs, including Hillside, initially participated, and two others joined later.

The Hillside team had an early win in the Winter League Championship in 1970/1. More sustained success came later when the Championship was won 11 times between 1977 and

Fig.116 *Southport and District Golf Association Winter League Champions 1977/8.*
From the left: Mike Pearson, Gordon Rimmer, Mike Walls, Rob Godley, Jack McLachlan the retired S&A professional, Ian McDiarmid and John McAlister.

2004 followed by a succession of second and third place finishes (Fig.116). The Summer Match Play competition was won on nine occasions and after a fallow period the Club again won the title in 2009. Further team success came in the Scratch Team 'Get Together' which has been won on ten occasions. By 1999 the Club had ten players with a handicap under two, and six of this group had a handicap under one (Fig.117).

Hillside won The Crosby Beacon in 1973, its inaugural year. The Beacon was an invitation pro-am tournament staged by the West Lancashire Club. Each of the 16 teams consisted of one professional and three amateurs. The format was an individual medal round with three gross scores to count, one of which must be the professional's. John Hewitt tied for the professional prize and the Hillside team finished seven strokes clear of Royal Liverpool, the runners-up. Further victories came in 1987, 1989, 1995, 1993 and 1998.

Fig.117 *Hillside Scratch Team and Trophies 1993. From the left rear: Andy Mather, Rob Maund, Graham Ackers, John Sciarrini, Alan Shaw, Duncan Swash, Richard Hennessey, Phil Kenyon, Paul Williams, Club Captain John Simmons, Rob Godley and Mark Howard. The trophies include West Lancashire's distinctive Crosby Beacon.*

Fig.118 *Liverpool and District Colts Challenge Cup Champions 1978. From the left: Neil Moir, Mike Walls, John Hepworth, Paul Buckels, Club Captain Eric Mawdesley, Rob Godley, Rob Maund, Sean Cowdry, Nick James, and Peter Allison.*

The Colts' Team

A Liverpool and District Colts Challenge Cup for 18 to 28-year-olds had been contested since the early 1930s and Hillside entered a team for the first time in 1965, but a lack of players led to them having to renege on its fixtures. Despite a request from Gordon Rimmer to revive the team in 1972, the Board was reluctant to consent until there was a guarantee that a team would be able to honour its commitments. Hillside had to wait until 1979 for its first success when the team defeated the holders Royal Liverpool in a final played at Hillside (Fig.118). To understand the magnitude and significance of this victory one has to appreciate the manner in which Royal Liverpool had previously dominated the championship. The members of Hillside's inexperienced team look back with gratitude to the devotion and energy of their organiser and 'chaperon' Joe Walsh and his ever-present sidekick John Mulvey. Rob Godley believes that this victory gave a new confidence, and an enduring impetus to inter-club golf at Hillside. A second colts' competition was introduced in 1983. The Renison Trophy recognises the contribution made by Bill Renison to colts' golf on Merseyside. Initially an early season scratch competition for teams of three, the Hillside trio won the inaugural event.

The Hillside squad had a second win in the Challenge Cup in 1984. It seems that the 1930's distinction between the scratch team and the colts was losing its significance and in 1985 the upper age limit was reduced to 26. New crops of colts were to win the championship in 1990 and 1991 and again in 1999.

Southport and District Golf Association Handicap League

The demand for competitive team golf extended beyond scratch teams and SDGA's summer league handicap match play tournament was launched in 1992. The competition was an instant success and after being the runner-up on four occasions the Hillside team were winners in 1998 and 2006.

The Ladies - with Pauline Horner

Hillside names began to appear on the County Association's silver ware. In 1968, **Mrs Edith Newsome**, the winner of nine club major competitions between 1948 and 1970, won the Lady Derby Challenge Cup (Fig.119). The local qualifying round was played at West Lancashire and the subsequent match-play rounds for the 16 qualifiers were played at Hillside. This marathon, completed in one week, involved two rounds a day. The weather was atrocious and Phil Irlam reports that Mrs Newsome, who did not like playing in waterproofs, was very grateful to the lady members for lending her changes of clothing. Ladies proudly recall that during this week a men's tournament was abandoned at neighbouring Royal Birkdale because of the weather. Edith, who was Lady Captain in 1972, was still winning ten years after her Lady Derby Cup success, taking the Veteran's Prize in 1977.

The opening of the new course coincided with the appearance of an exceptional young girl golfer at Hillside - **Carline Eckersley**. Her father was appointed as the Club's caterer in 1968. Carline, then a 14-year-old, had played the game from the age of 12 and had already won the Welsh Northern Counties under 15 Years Championship.

It was a time when there were few girls with handicaps, and

Fig.119 *Edith Newsome. A major force in ladies' golf at Hillside.*

Carline's arrival at Hillside coincided with a Lancashire Ladies' Golf Association initiative to promote the involvement of girls in the game. The Lancashire Junior Championship had been played once in 1950, but was not competed for again until 1969. This handicap event was revived and played at Formby Ladies, and Carline, then 15-years-old and 15 handicap, won with a gross score of 87. No entry fee was charged and after the championship the competitors were given a group lesson by the Formby professional. Lancashire started to fund girls' coaching for the first time. Bunty Stephens was the driving force behind this initiative. Carline benefited enormously from this support and the facilities available to her at Hillside. As a memento the Ladies' Section presented her with an inscribed silver spoon. At the presentation the Lady Captain told the members that: 'We have great hopes for this young lady.' She was to win the revived county championship in three of its first four years. Selection for Lancashire came for 16-year-old Carline in the Northern Women's County Championship played at Hillside in 1970, when she won three of her four matches. The Ladies' Section agreed to pay for her Lancashire uniform. After playing well in the English Girls' Championship, in the same year, she was selected to play for the England team in the Girls' Home Internationals at Llandudno

In 1971, Carline won the English Girls' Championship, a victory that gained her selection to again play for England in the Girls' Home Internationals at North Berwick, where she won two of her three singles matches (Fig.120). Her defeat was at the hands of Scotland's Cathy Panton, who was to become a distinguished professional. The Ladies' Section presented her with an inscribed gold watch to mark her success in the championship.

Her handicap came down to one and competing at senior level she reached the quarter-finals of the English Women's Championship which was played at Royal Liverpool. In 1972 she was defeated by Ann Irvin, one of England's top lady golfers, in the final of the Lancashire Championship and in 1974 the same opponent again defeated her.

Carline won the Best Scratch Score competition in each of her four years at Hillside, her best score being 76. She was also able to successfully play in medals but Club rules prevented her playing in its other major competitions. Her father was appointed as caterer at Burnley Golf Club in 1972, and this became Carline's club, but after the mid 1970s she seems to have disappeared from the club, county and international golfing scene.

The honours board shows that in the decade following Carline's four years of posting the Best Scratch Score, **Mrs Mavis Curtis** took the title five times whilst Mrs Nola Sawyer, who was Lady Captain in 1976 and 1990, won it on three occasions.

Pat Smillie then won the trophy five times between 1981 and 1986, with a best score of 73, still the lowest winning total. She was the Hillside lady member with the all-time strongest golf CV. Pat had begun to play the game as a nine-year-old in her native Scotland. When the family moved to Yorkshire she became a member at Pannal Golf Club with a handicap of 24. She made rapid progress and was to play for Yorkshire for ten years, winning the Yorkshire Championship twice. She was twice the holder of the English Girls' Championship and represented her adopted country at all levels including playing for the full international side.

Fig.120 *Carline Eckersley. A caricature by local hairdresser Tom Rooney.*

In 1980, when Pat was 18, her parents moved to live in Formby. She joined Hillside and continued to play representative golf, whilst studying sports science at Liverpool Polytechnic (Fig.121). Within the Club she won the Lady Captain's Prize in 1986, but deliberately restricted her opportunities to win trophies, other than the Scratch Trophy, in order that others might have their names on the honours boards. It was shortly after this time that she played as a professional on the European Tour for four years. In 1994 she became one of the few lady club professionals in the country when she was appointed to Wilton Golf Club on Teeside. Pat rapidly earned a regional reputation as a coach and is now the English Ladies' Golf Association's national junior coach and its Director of Coaching.

After Pat's departure, the honours boards were dominated by the unparalleled achievements of **Mrs Bernie Kenyon**. She joined the Club in 1980 having taken the game up in her 40th year. Within six years she reduced her handicap to four and she was never to have a handicap greater than five for the next 20 years (Fig.122). In a 21 year run from 1987 her name appears as a winner in the annual contest to record the Best Scratch Score in all but one year, sharing the title on four occasions. Her best score was a 75, equalling the ladies' par. Additionally she has won the Lady Captain's Prize, the Sherrington Bowl seven times, the Smith Cup on three occasions and the Lucas Trophy.

Fig.121 *(Below) The Home Internationals at Whittington Barracks 1986. Pat Smillie is the second from the right.*

Fig.122 *(Left) Bernie Kenyon. An exceptional golf late developer.*

1996 saw this extraordinarily consistent golfer also win the Veterans' Prize. Not surprisingly Bernie has been selected to play for the Lancashire Seniors' team. She played in the Lancashire team that regularly won the six Northern Counties' Richardson Trophy.

A new name, **Mrs Abby Sanderson**, appeared on the Club's Best Scratch Score Board in 2008. This newcomer to Hillside gold paint ended the year with three of the ladies' seven major trophies.

After a long struggle to raise a scratch team to play in the Lancashire County Golf Association championship Hillside did eventually compete at this level, but although enjoying some success the Club has not had the playing strength to make an impact in the competition, or to consistently enter a team.

The Lancashire Handicap Shield had been introduced in 1928 for players with a handicap under 24, but only one player with a single figure handicap is allowed to play in a team. There are seven players in a team and the winners of each of the four divisions of the county meet in the semi-finals and final. The initial stage involves 14 matches, seven at home and seven away. In 1990, the Hillside team qualified for the play off at Ormskirk, where, on a day that turned out to be the hottest day of the year, the team managed to qualify for the September county finals at Swinton Park. Here a strong Lancaster team were beaten in the morning semi-final and

Fig.123 *Lancashire Ladies' Handicap Trophy Champions 1990. Back row from the left: Rita Abberley, Marjorie Ostenfeld, Jean Hough, Olive Cutts, Sheila Smith-Crallan, Anita Cranswick and Muriel Moss, front row: Janet Hewitt, Barbara Carter, Jean Priestley (team captain), Lady Captain Nola Sawyer, Jenny Davis and Edna Giddens. Seven members of this team have served as lady captain.*

Great Harwood in the afternoon final. This was Hillside ladies' first success in winning a Lancashire County Golf Association team trophy (Fig.123).

The Bronze Shield was introduced by the County in 2004 and is played for by a team of five ladies with handicaps between 21 and 36. Hillside has entered a team for this competition since its inauguration, initially under the captaincy of Mrs Ann Turnbull (Fig.124). The following year Mrs Margaret Parkes took over and after two years the baton was passed to Mrs Pauline Horner. In both 2007 and 2008 the Hillside team finished as winners of the south-west Lancashire area and in 2007 it won through to the area finals but lost to S&A who went on to win the Shield. From 2009 Jan Maund took over the role of captain.

There is an additional ladies' team, which provides informal experience of inter-club match play golf for those not in one of the teams playing within the framework of the county competitions.

The Juniors

Up to the 1970s there had been little organised junior golf. The number of junior members was small and the majority of them were the sons and daughters of members. Competitions were rare and there were severe restrictions as to when they could play. There was a sea change in attitude and the Handicap Committee actively encouraged the juniors.

One of the early beneficiaries to this change was Steve Rooke (Fig.125). He won the Lancashire Boys' Championship in 1967, playing for the Lancashire Colts' Team against Yorkshire in 1968 and gaining England Boys' International honours in the same year, and in 1971, he represented England at youth level. Although he had reduced his handicap to three by the time he was 15, Mike Pearson did not enjoy such an outstanding junior career as Steve. Nevertheless, in 1965, as a 17-year-old he did have a gross score of 67. Another junior success story was that of Rob Godley. He won the Liverpool and District Boys' Challenge Trophy in 1972. In the same year he also won the Southport and District Perpetual Boys' Challenge Trophy for 11 to 17-year-olds, a trophy won by Duncan Swash in the following year. There was then a gap until Phil Kenyon won it in 1988. Phillip also played for Lancashire and England Schoolboys. Mark

Prue played for Lancashire boys in 1997 and won the *Daily Mail* Junior Trophy at Valderama. In 2001, Andy Sumner became the first Hillside member to become Lancashire Boys' Champion since Steve Rooke. He had played in the prestigious Boys' Amateur Championship at Hillside in the previous year and qualified for the final rounds of the Brabazon at Royal Birkdale.

Fig.124 *Lancashire Ladies' Bronze Shield team 2004. From the left: Karen Nolan, Ann Turnbull, Pauline Bennett, Jan Maund and Margaret Parkes.*

A Hillside Boys' Open tournament was introduced in 1975. This 36 holes event has gone from strength to strength and is frequently over-subscribed. Home competitors have enjoyed some success in this event. It was won, with a nett score of 144, by John Sciarrini in 1980 and in 1985 by Alister McDiarmid. Adam Hansen was the winner in 1997 and 1998. Ryan Gillespie was a home winner in 1999 and Richie Blundell in 2001. In the following year Richie fought his way through to the finals of the *Daily Telegraph* Junior Golfer of the Year in South Africa. In 2008 Greg Monk won the SDGA Junior Championship, the only Hillside boy to achieve this to date (Fig.126). In the following year Zain Wild, the Junior Captain, played in the Lancashire under 16 Championship and for the county boys' team and the county under 18 years team (Fig.127).

Fig.125 *Boys having a group lesson c.1962. From the left: Robert Graham, James Graham, Joe Millard, Steve Rooke and Mike Pearson.*

Fig.126 *Greg Monk, Junior Captain 2008.*

A Junior Committee was put in place in 1980 and stalwarts such as Bill Ackers, Gordon Hughes, John Mulvey, Tom Murray, John Nelson, Gordon Pearson, David Prue, Joe Walsh, John Sciarrini, Mrs Sheelah Foulds, who was chairman for six years, served on it with distinction. Gordon Rimmer, who was particularly dedicated to this committee, was also its chairman. His greatest concern was to ensure that Hillside youngsters had a proper grounding in golfing practice and etiquette.

The Committee put into place a programme of club competitions. The **H.S. Collinge Trophy** was first contested in 1980, the **Chairman's Prize** in 1981, the **Junior Committee Cup** in 1982, the **Professional's Prize** in 1983, and the **250 Club Trophy** in 1987. The **Junior Trophy**, the **John Burton Trophy**, the **Captain's Prize**, the **Lady Captain's Prize**, the **Denis Nutter Trophy**, the **Kelsey Bowl**, the **Gordon Rimmer Trophy** and the **Harold James Lads and Dads Trophy** were later added to the prize table (Fig.128). The majority of the competitions are now played on Sundays at 10.30am. A programme of informal inter-club junior matches also evolved. 1980 saw the launch of an annual match with Bingley St. Ives; the Guy Lawson Trophy for this fixture was introduced in 2005. Fixtures with Bootle and others were also played on a 'social' basis.

In 1990 Southport and District Golf Association introduced a Junior Team Trophy for under 18-year-olds. Although Hillside didn't have a win in the first eight years of this competition it has since become the most successful club with eight wins in the last 12 years. In 2001 the team went on to win a regional competition and qualified to participate in the national finals a feat repeated in 2008 and 2009.

Fig.127 *Zain Wild, Junior Captain 2010.*

Following the success of Carline Eckersley, Hillside unearthed occasional promising girl golfers without being able to develop a strong group. Angela Canavan, a member's daughter, was the first girl to win the Hillside Junior Trophy in 1981, and was able to retain it in the following year. She also competed successfully in regional events. Unfortunately Angela was lost to the Club when the family left the district.

About ten years later Jane Hancock, whose parents were enthusiastic members, joined the Club as an 11-year-old and was given a handicap of 36. Taught by Brian Seddon, she dropped 11 shots in 1994, got down into single figures and won the Pleasington Junior Open Title (Fig.129). She became a member of the Lancashire girls' squad, and played at the various age levels of the Lancashire girls' team and as such was coached by Jane Forrest, a former European Tour player. Jane later helped with coaching girls at Hillside, before moving to the south of England. She retained her membership and is an occasional visitor to the Club.

In recent years the junior competitions have been open to both boys and girls and Laura Green, Lucinda Mawdesley and Haley Nolan have all won one of the junior trophies. Girls have also played regularly in the junior team, whilst Laura Green and her father Graham were the first mixed-sex pair to win the Lads and Dads Trophy.

Fig.128 *Juniors' presentation table.*

Fig.129 *Brian Seddon coaching Jane Hancock c.1998.*

Chapter Ten
Social Hillside
1967 - 2010

Organised golf at Hillside was not limited to the competitive teams already described, but came in a variety of other formats.

Team Matches

Captain's Matches

The Reigning Captains' Shield, a competition contested by the coastal clubs between Southport and Liverpool along with Ormskirk and Wigan, was won by a Hillside pairing in 1995, 1997, 1999 and 2009. Captain's team matches continued to be played as social fixtures, five or six Sunday fixtures being played annually. These were definitely occasions for an 'honourable draw' and a late pass.

Seniors' Team

There was an appetite within the Club for opportunities for inter-club match play golf to be extended to seniors/veterans. Similar stirrings were occurring in other local clubs. Senior golf in the Southport district has grown informally. Initially S&A wrote to Hillside in 1977 informing it that a team catering for retired members had been set up and were to play a team from West Lancashire. They asked Hillside whether it was interested in having a similar match. The Board referred the query to a man with the perfect credentials to formulate Hillside's response - Tom Johnson, a past captain with experience as joint secretary of the Club. A team was raised and played against S&A and West Lancashire. Tom also arranged a match with Huyton and Prescott.

In 1980, Bob Woods briefly took on the role of organising the Veterans' Section and Grange Park and Childwall were added to the list. David Hamer, a long serving club member who, although in his 80s, was still a fiercely competitive player, replaced Woods as organiser in 1982 and two years later Hesketh was added to the fixtures and caused a stir by including a former English Amateur Champion and a veteran Ryder Cup player in its team. David Cutbill took over the organisation of the section and additional matches with Haydock Park were played. In 1989, Murdo MacLeod took over as Seniors' Section organiser from David Cutbill, who had not been able to play because of ill health. The fixture list was expanded to include Ormskirk, who had just ventured into veteran golf.

Local clubs had not followed the approach adopted in other areas, where veterans' leagues have been set up. Matches were played on a social basis, with each club determining its own fixture list. Competition can be quite fierce on the course but the result in the clubhouse continues to be an 'honourable draw'. By 2008 the Seniors' Section was experiencing difficulty in raising a team of 16 to fulfil its fixtures and the size of the team was reduced to 12. By 2009, under the leadership of Syd Cobb and Tom Murray, the section appears once again to be in rude health and Formby Golf Club has been added to the fixture list (Fig.130).

Fig.130 *Seniors' Team V. Formby 2010. From the left back: Derek Hillsdon, Ken Roche, Jimmy Helm, Brian Kenyon, Alan Croft, Tom Farley, Jim Fitzpatrick, Graham Jones, Tom Murray, Syd Cobb and Brian Dean.*

Domestically the season opened in spring with the **Memorial Trophy** and closed in autumn with the **Wilkinson Trophy**, the seniors' oldest trophy, which was donated by Walter Wilkinson. Still playing in his 90s, Walter had been a member of the Club for over 70 years. Gerry Attwood, one of the strongest players in the Veterans' Section, became Club chairman in 1986. In an attempt develop club spirit he proposed that the veterans should play matches against the ladies and the juniors. The match with the ladies, for whom the veterans provided refreshments, was first played in 1987. It was deemed to be so successful that a second annual match was added. David Cutbill later donated the **Cutbill Shield** for this annual competition.

Charity, Society and Sponsored Golf

The **Freddie Veale Pro/Am** was played, in conjunction with the Liverpool and District Golf Alliance, in the late 1970s in order to mark the extraordinary contribution that he had made both at Hillside and to professional and amateur golf outside the Club. Played on a Sunday it was supported by some 50 professionals and each team of four was completed by a member drawn from each of three handicap bands (Fig.131). It was a 'Freddie Veale event' bringing members together in a way in which other competitions do not and at the same time supporting professional golfers.

In 1980 the Club first staged an annual Pro-Am in aid of the Lancashire Association of Boys' Clubs. Initially the **Frankie Vaughan Boys' Club Pro-Am Classic**, it later became the **Bill Beaumont Pro-Am Golf Classic** and tens of thousands of pounds have been raised. Regional professionals have supported the event, competing for the professional prize. Rugby Union star and media personality Bill Beaumont's day is still part of the Club calendar and continues to draw strong support, particularly from sponsors in east Lancashire (Fig.132). Since the year 2000 the **Alan Hansen Golf Classic** for teams of four has also been played annually at Hillside. Alan, a former professional footballer and now a distinguished football pundit, has raised considerable sums for charity through this event.

Society of Liverpool Golf Club Captains

Hillside captains continued to support the Society of Liverpool Golf Club Captains (Fig.133). Former World War II bomber pilot, Bill (Wally) Allison DFC, won the Annual Competition (nett prize) in 1973. In 1987, Dr. Fred Wilson became the first Hillside winner of the scratch competition.

Fig.131 *Freddie Veale Pro-Am 1978 Programme.*

Fig.132 *Bill Beamont's Charity Day. Bill is on the extreme right*

On the same day John McAlister won the Spaven (veterans) Trophy. Their two scores along with that of Reg Smith won the Leverhulme Salver. George Owen won the Spaven Trophy in 1992 and, in the same year, tied for the Benstead Trophy, for three cards on the annual outing. Derek Anderson won the Hayco Trophy, the annual competition (the nett prize) in 1996, his year as captain. In the following year John Simmons won the Benstead Trophy. In 2001, when Bryan Greenwood was Captain of the Society, the Annual Meeting was held at Hillside, but it seems that home advantage was insufficient to produce a Hillside winner.

Society of Liverpool Lady Golf Club Captains

It was in this era that lady members at Hillside began to make an increased impact beyond the confines of domestic club affairs. Mrs Eileen Bankes was elected to the captaincy of the Liverpool Society of Lady Golf Captains in 1964, and she was the Lancashire Ladies' Captain in 1968. Mrs Pat Dickinson shared the duties of Lancashire Competition Secretary between 1971 and 1974, whilst Mrs Rita Abberley, the 1980 Lady Captain, was Captain of the Liverpool Society in 1988, a position held by the Club's 2006 Lady Captain, Mrs Pam Green, in 2009. The Society's annual meeting was held at Hillside during this year and the home team won the competition for the Hodson Salver (Fig.134).

Ad Hoc Golfing Groups

Hillside members have come together for golf outside the formal Club framework. Perhaps the most significant of these 'institutions' is the long-established **SMU (Sunday Morning Union)**. Founded by John Brignall and Jeff White in the 1950s, it meets at 8am on a Sunday morning. Many members have got a weekly 'fix' of competitive golf playing in the SMU and tall tales are told of their achievements.

Some 33 years ago Hillside also spawned the **Natterjacks**, founder members include John Coyle and Gerry Brunskill. This group is predominantly made up of Hillside members and plays

Fig.133 *Hillside Captains outside the R&A Clubhouse, St Andrews 1985. From the left: Dennis Woods, Reg Smith, Roy Allan, Bill Backhouse, Jim Mullen, John McAlister and Dr Fred Wilson.*

an annual game on the course. The Natterjacks migrate on an annual golf excursion, with their destination frequently being Scotland.

The Rusty Zips is a group of over 65-year-olds who play on Tuesdays and Fridays. Founded by Stan Goodwin, the oldest member is 88-year-old John Godley. Only nine holes are played and the record score is held by Hillside's rules' expert

Fig.134 *Society of Liverpool Lady Golf Captain's Day at Hillside 2009. From the left: Mrs Margaret Parkes, Mrs Jean Priestley, Mrs Jenny Davis, Mr David Dixon (Captain), Mrs Pam Green (Captain of Captains), Mr. Olive Cutts, Mrs Janet Perkins (Lady Captain)*

Johnny Ball with 26 Stableford points. Tea follows the competition, when there is a redistribution of pension money.

Since 2001 an annual competition, followed by a dinner, has been played for **The Moss Pipe** to perpetuate the memory of popular Hillside member George Moss.

The **Wayfarers' Golfing Society** was established in 1950 (Fig.135). The roots of this thriving invitation society appear to have been in the Hillside Club, which is still heavily represented in its membership and its printed membership book shows that the first of its four annual golf meetings is always played at Hillside. The AGM and annual dinner are also held at Hillside, whilst the clubhouse is designated as the society's headquarters.

Since the early 1970s many Club members have also been involved in a golf society –**SAGS** – which was founded and organised by Alan Whittaker. They have supported its annual golf week in Scotland and attended its Burn's golf day and haggis supper at Hillside.

Rather more exotic was Harold James' International Challenge Match, which he described as a **Mini-Ryder Cup Series**. It was contested on an annual basis between 1995 and 1998 by a team that he selected, consisting principally of Hillside members, and one from a Florida golf and country club.

Commercially Sponsored Tournaments

Both men and women have prospered in such events. In 1974 professional John Hewitt and his partners, who included Dr. Fred Wilson, came second in the Yankee Bar pro-am played in Denmark.

In 1976, Mrs Pam Roberts (nee Rook), a member since the 1930s, whose handicap had been as low as ten, qualified with Marjorie Ostenfeld to compete in the Finals of the Volkswagon Grand Prix Amateur Golf Championship at Turnberry. Mrs Nola Sawyer, the Lady Captain, joined them for their two nights stay.

In 1986 Gordon Rimmer and Andy Mather won the area final of the Rioja Golf Championship, which was played at Hillside.

Extraordinarily Hillside provided three of the 12 English qualifiers for The Rover Cup Four Nations Golf Tournament at La Manga Spain in 1989. This was from a field of 100,000 original entrants. Winners of the preliminary club rounds from both handicap bands played at one of the 'Royal' courses in each of the four home countries to determine the composition of the four 12-strong international teams. The ladies in the Hillside trio, who qualified at Royal Birkdale, were Mrs Jenny Davis and Mrs Jean Henessey and the man was Brian Kenyon (Fig.136). The competition, hosted by Tony Jacklin, was played over six days and the Welsh team was the eventual winner. Brian's record of winning four and halving two of his six matches gained him selection for a Great Britain team to play in America. Sadly the financial collapse of the Rover car group prevented this happening.

Fig.135 *Wayfarer's Golfing Society 1966. There are more than a dozen Hillside members in this group.*

Fig.136 *Rover Cup Four Nations Tournament, La Manga 1989.*
The English team including Jean Hennesey and Jenny Davis to Tony Jacklin's left,
and Brian Kenyon second from the right.

After winning the qualifying round of the Daily Mail Foursomes at Hillside in 1993, Bernie Kenyon and Mrs Sheila Smith-Crallan survived seven regional match play games before qualifying for the two-day finals at Lindrick Golf Club.

Social Hillside

The Club continued to support an active programme of social events; a calendar of more than 20 is published in the 'member's directory'. The lapsed men's annual clubhouse dinner was reintroduced in 1970, but the overall trend was towards more mixed events. One function that has been lost has been the children's Christmas party. For the captain the pleasure, or ordeal, of being Father Christmas is over. Only 12 children attended in 2001 and it was decided to discontinue the event.

From 1967 the ladies presented an annual pantomime, originally performed solely for the ladies. Initially organised by Edith Newsome, an enthusiastic member of the local operatic society, and based on a golf theme, this popular show was later produced by Mrs Joan Brown, who was succeeded by Olive Cutts (Fig.137). The annual pantomime is no longer presented but perhaps its spirit lives on in the fancy dress of themed dinners.

Hillside could well be unique amongst golf clubs in having a mixed backgammon league. This winter competition was another baby of Alan Whittaker, a long-standing member

Fig.137 *The Cinderella cast 1987.*
Back row from the left: Marjorie Ostenfeld, Gertrude Tebble, Gwen Rimmer, Barbara Carter, Shirley Allan, Edith Newsome, Olive Cutts, Enid Naylor and Edna Giddens.

The New Year's Eve dance traditionally sees the introduction of the new captain whose drive in is the occasion for a party the following morning. In 2010 the Lady Captain's drive-in was halted by the weather. After the ladies arrived at the clubhouse there was a heavy snow fall which carpeted the course. Magically a sledge was available to carry her to the 1st tee. Sheelah then slalomed across the snow under the arch of clubs held by shivering past captains but the effort was in vain and the official drive-in was postponed (Fig.138).

Having two snooker tables ensures that there is ample opportunity for casual players, whilst they also allow the more serious players of the snooker section to complete a programme of competitive matches and tournaments. It is interesting to note that several winners also figure strongly on the golf honours' boards.

without pretensions as a golfer, although he did once win a glass sweet bowl. Alan was to leave his idiosyncratic mark on Hillside in many ways, including as a photographer.

Sporting Celebrity Members

Hillside has a tradition of welcoming footballers as members. From the early 1960s George Bromilow, a local boy, was a member. George played for the Great Britain team in the Melbourne Olympic Games and had a prolific goal scoring record as an amateur for Southport in the Football League (Fig.139). In more recent years, a number of current and former professional footballers have been members. They include Alan Hansen, Kenny Dalglish, Ian Callaghan, Geoff Strong, Jim Beglin, Mike Newall and Kevin Sheedy. Not surprisingly, the honours boards testify to the fact that they tend to be competitive golfers. They also recognise that 'celebrity' is a burden they carry and they have used it for the service of the Club, making presentations to the juniors, speaking at members' dinners and organising and participating in charity events.

English Rugby Union international Pat Quinn, a winner of the Malies' Trophy in 1969, was a Lancashire team mate of Gordon Rimmer, and later played Rugby League for Leeds. After retiring from the game he became a rugby correspondent for a national newspaper. His life was tragically cut short in a road accident, when returning north from Twickenham.

Hillside's sporting celebrities also included George Leigh, whose name appeared several times on the honours boards in the early 1970s. George was a professional motorcycle racer whose reputation was made on the TT circuit of the Isle of Man. He had a motor cycle shop on Eastbank Street Bridge. A current member and another enthusiastic motor cycle racer is Derek Vaux. This septuagenarian and former Clubman Trophy competitor claims that he still powers his MV Agusta at over 180 mph around the Aintree circuit.

Club Newsletter

A Club newsletter, *Hillside Links: The Journal* of the Hillside Golf Club, provides social glue to help secure the cohesion of the Club. It benefited from the journalistic skills of its founder and editor John Nelson, an experienced and skilled professional. The *Journal* highlights the activities of all the sections of the Club, contains special features, and relies on many contributors. Text is enhanced by the excellence of the accompanying illustrations; the Club has an exceptional well of talented individuals in this field. Nigel Dixon's contribution to Hillside as an artist and a photographer has set the benchmark high. The *Journal*, now edited by Geoff Lord, has attracted sponsorship from members and consistently achieves professional production standards.

Fig.138 *(Top Left)* Lady Captain Sheelah's Drive-in, 'Take One' 2010.

Fig.139 *(Left)* George Bromilow receiving the Captain's Prize from Vic Bateson 1972.

Chapter Eleven
Hillside Centenary
2011

The jewel in Hillside's centenary crown is the award by the R&A of the Amateur Championship, Britain's most prestigious amateur tournament. The championship was born on this coast from an initiative of the Royal Liverpool Club in 1885 and quickly came under the auspices of the R&A. The West Lancashire and Formby clubs joined Royal Liverpool among the 24 original subscribers towards the cost of the trophy (Fig.140). The names of these clubs are engraved in a panel on the cup.

It might seem extraordinary but in the years between the World Wars the Amateur Championship attracted more newspaper column inches than the Open Championship; the Amateur Champions were better known than their professional counterparts and the Amateur Championship was the more financially self reliant of the two. Television has played a large part in reversing this state of affairs and elevating professional golf to stellar status. To succeed as a tournament professional is now the aspiration of young amateurs and what a launching pad this championship affords them. The winner has an invitation to play in the Open Championship and the US Masters. Recent winners of the Amateur Championship have been younger than their predecessors. When it was played at Formby in 2009, the winner was the youngest ever champion, Matteo Manassero, a 16-year-old Italian schoolboy. Having qualified for the Open Championship he made the cut, won the silver medal for the leading amateur, and extraordinarily, despite a late slump, finished in 13th place overall. After surviving all four rounds of the US Masters at Augusta, he again received the award as the leading amateur. He was then invited to play in several professional tournaments

Fig.140 *The Amateur Championship at Hillside 1979. The trophy awaits the winner.*

129

Fig.141 *EGU Home Internationals Championship 2009. Spectators following one of the matches on the 17th hole.*

and, shortly after his 17th birthday, he turned professional, and secured lucrative sponsorship deals and soon set a record as the youngest player to win a European Tour event. The 2010 Amateur Champion at St Andrews was 20-year-old Korean Jin Jeong, a newcomer to links golf, whose preparation included practice and play at Hillside, where he shot a round of 63. Jin went on to take the silver medal and finish joint 14th in the Open Championship. He will retain his amateur status until after he plays at Augusta in 2011.

Hosting the Amateur Championship in 2011 puts Hillside in the forefront of amateur golf in this country. Some of the young golfers taking part will probably go on to become stars of the professional circuits. The Amateur Championship will be an opportunity for spectators to accompany the players around the Hillside course, unimpeded by barriers or ropes (Fig.141). For clubs such as Hillside it seems that hosting prestigious amateur tournaments, under the auspices of the R&A and EGU, has superseded the major professional events held on their courses in former years. The Ladies' Golf Union has invited the Club to host the Ladies' Home International Championship at Hillside during the Centenary Year.

Fig.142 *Jimmy Tarbuck. The catalyst for the centenary match with Coombe Hill.*

Fig.143 *A club badge to celebrate 100 years*

Golf Monthly celebrates its centenary in 2011 and has chosen to ask Hillside to host its celebrations in which other centenary clubs will be invited to share. Additionally, there will be a Centenary Challenge Match with Coombe Hill, also founded in 1911. The catalyst for this fixture, which will involve two days of competition at home and away, is comedian Jimmy Tarbuck, who is a member of both clubs (Fig.142). Jimmy, who played regularly at Hillside with former Liverpool footballers Ian Callaghan and Geoff Strong, was a considerable golfer. When playing in the English Open Over 35s Championship at West Lancashire in 1992, his second round score of 75 in a gale force wind was described in *Amateur Golfer* as '...one of the rounds of the championship.'

A rich programme of events has been planned for the centenary year. There will be two-day 36 holes Centenary Trophy Competitions for ladies and for men, Centenary Invitations will be followed by dinners in the marquee. The ladies are to have an exchange day with Royal Lytham, whilst the juniors will celebrate 30 years of the annual match with Bingley, with a special fixture open to anyone who has ever played in this match. The last golfing event of the year will involve turning back the clock for a Centenary Hickory Club Challenge.

Club centenary celebrations will not be confined to the course and the clubhouse will host a number of special events. The marquee planned to be in place for the Amateur Championship will also be used for this programme and the centenary badge will act as a reminder throughout the year (Fig. 143).

Hillside has upgraded its course and clubhouse and is a club prepared to meet the challenges of the future (Fig.144). The staff in every department will strive to ensure a memorable centenary year, and to continue to offer a first class service to the members and visitors. It is the secretariat which deals with members and visitors queries and concerns.

Fig.144 *The clubhouse from the 18th Hole 2009.*
The removal of the iconic chimney was linked to the changes that had occured within the clubhouse.

Fig.145 *The Secretariat 2010.*
From the left: Mrs Jo Palmer, Secretary/Manager Simon Newland and Mrs Val Charlesworth.

Fig.146 *Martin Twist and his team 2010.*

The staff in every department will strive to ensure a memorable centenary year, and to continue to offer a first class service to the members and visitors. It is the secretariat which deals with members and visitors queries and concerns. The team provide the human face behind the operation of the increasingly complex information technology regime, which has become the common place of golf clubs (Fig.145).

The Club has been fortunate that it has had the services of two outstanding and long-serving head greenkeepers, Ted MacAvoy (1947-1972) and Martin Twist (1987-), during the last half century. They have led teams which have transformed what was probably the most nondescript course on the south-west Lancashire dune coast into a links course with a well-merited international reputation (Fig.146).

Long-service has been a feature of the Club's bar staff. The present incumbents include Val Preston who started work at the Club in 1980 (Fig 147). Hillside has a magnificent first floor dining room, overlooking the course, and the catering staff has earned the Club a justified reputation for quality service (Fig.148).

Captaincy of the Club requires a considerable degree of commitment. The number of domestic functions, involving both members and visitors, that require the presence of the captain continues to grow. In addition the captain has to represent Hillside at numerous functions away from the Club. He is a figurehead and helps to set standards, but, after a year in office he is a past captain and it is claimed that '...there is nothing quite so past (Fig.149)'. The Lady Captain also contributes substantially to the life of the Club and particularly the Ladies' Section (Fig.150).

Fig.147 *Some of the Club's longest serving bar staff.*

Fig.148 *Staff from the catering supplier contracted to the Club.*

Fig.149 Captains 2010. Front row from the left: W.C. Backhouse, R.J. Smith, K.N. Owen, P. Molloy, J.D. Giddens, Dr. C.F. Wilson, R.M. Allan, B.L. Greenwood, G.C. Hinds, G. Brunskill, G.C. Kendrick, G.D. Anderson, D.M. Cox, J.J. Simmons, C.E. Pennington, G.P. Owen, D. Lanigan, G.A. Charnock, I.A. McDiarmid, J.A. Proctor, B.G. Crilly, K.J. Parkinson and J.A. Taylor.

Fig.150 *Lady Captains 2010. Front Row L to R: Mrs Seward, Mrs Geoghegan, Mrs Hennessy, Mrs Parkes, Mrs Cranswick, Mrs Greenwood, Mrs Sawyer, Mrs Abberley, Mrs Giddens. Middle Row L to R: Mrs Naylor, Mrs Davis, Mrs Allan, Mrs Marshall, Mrs Cutts, Mrs Proctor, Mrs Cobb, Mrs Crilly, Mrs Willcocks, Mrs Taylor. Back Row L to R: Mrs Foulds, Mrs Perkins, Mrs Leonard, Mrs Anderson, Mrs Green, Mrs Newton, Mrs Hewitt, Mrs Priestley, Mrs Hough, Mrs Turnbull*

The captains may be the public faces of Hillside Golf Club; however, it is in the Board Room, where the directors meet, that the responsibility for the conduct of the affairs of Hillside Golf Club Limited resides (Fig.151).

'Tale'piece

Club histories commemorate the past. Golf clubs are places of memories and every member will have a store of reminiscences. Has Lady Captain Rita Abberley been telling 1980 Captain Gordon Lindsay about her mother's 1973 captaincy (Fig.152)? What were Gordon Rimmer and Harold James celebrating in 1996 (Fig.153)? Well it seems that they were both interviewed for membership on the same evening in 1946 and later shared a Whitsuntide mixed foursomes introduction to competitive golf at Hillside. The pair marked their 50 years of membership by jointly presenting a trophy for this event in 1996. Their century is the stuff of tales, as are the memories of many others, but it would require another book to tell them all.

I intended that this centenary story should close with the photograph of Rimmer and James, but Gordon and Harold would understand and applaud my choice of the final image (Fig.154).

Fig.151 *The board room following the clubhouse refurbishment of 2008*

Fig 152 *A Collection of Captains, 1980. Esther Massam, the 1973 Lady Captain, with her daughter Rita Abberley, the Lady Captain, and Club Captain George Lindsay.*

Fig.153 *'Tale'piece 1996. Gordon Rimmer (left) and Harold James celebrate their 50 years of Hillside membership.*

Fig.154 *The Future. Eight members of the Junior Team 'sporting' shirts provided by a donation from the 250 Club. The team were again the winners of the SDGA Junior Championship in 2010.*

Bibliography

Beherend, John,	*The Story of the Amateur Golf Championship 1885-1995*, (1995)
Beherend, J., Lewis, P.N. & Mackie, K.,	*Champions & Guardians, The Royal & Ancient Golf Club 1884-1939*, (2001)
Browning, R.H.K.,	'Southport of the Seven Courses' *Golfing*, May 1926.
Birtill, David,	*Celebrating the County Golf Union: Lancashire Links 1910-2010*, (2010)
Childs, Walter, (mss.),	*Notes on the Origin and Early History of Southport and Ainsdale Golf Club*, (1946)
Cotton, Henry,	*This Game of Golf*, (1948)
Coyne, Barry,	*The West Lancashire Golf Club, A History of Golf at Blundellsands*, (2008)
Dabell, Norman,	*How we Won the Open, The Caddies' Stories*, (1990)
Davies, Patricia,	*A History of Formby Ladies' Golf Club*, (1996)
Dixon, Nancy,	*Hesketh Ladies*, (1989)
Edwards, L.,	*The West Lancashire Golf Club, Blundellsands*, (1973)
Foster, Harry,	*Links Along the Line: The Story of the Development of Golf Between Southport and Liverpool*, (1995 & 2009)
Foster, Harry,	*Annals of the Hesketh Golf Club 1885-2000*, (2001)
Foster, Harry,	*Southport and Ainsdale: The Golfers' Club*, (2006)
Hilton, Harold,	'Where to Golf' *ABC Guide to Towns and Pleasure Resorts upon the Lancashire and Yorkshire Railway*, (c.1910)
Irlam, Philip,	*A Lively Octogenarian: Hillside Golf Club 1911-1991*, (1993)
Johnson, A.J.D.,	*The Royal Birkdale Golf Club*, (1989)
Leece, Geoffrey,	*The Society of Liverpool Golf Captains: A Celebration of one Hundred Years 1908-2008*, (2008)
Mair, Lewine,	*One Hundred Years of Women's Golf*, (1992)
Nicklaus, Jack,	*Jack Nicklaus: My Story*, (1997)
Nickson, E.A.,	*The Lytham Century and Beyond 1886-2000*, (2000)
Steel, D. & Lewis, P.N.,	*Traditions & Change, The Royal and Ancient Golf Club 1939-2004*, (2004)
Tew, Tom	'Golf Courses and Wildlife Files' *The Golf Club Secretary*, January 2004.
Thomas, I.S.,	*Formby Golf Club 1884-1972*, (1972)
Tiffany, Sylvia,	*Lancashire Ladies County Golf Association: 100 Years 1900-2000*, (1999)
Wilson, E.,	*A Gallery of Women Golfers*, (1961)
Hillside Golf Club,	*Minutes of the Board, Green, Handicap (Golf Administration), House, Social, Strategic and Finance Committees*, (1923-2010)
Southport Reference Library,	
	Southport Visiter, (1906-2010)
	Proceedings of the Southport Town Council (1906-1974)
	Census Enumerators' Returns (1901 & 1911)

The Honours Board
Captains

1919	R Mook	1950	B Turner	1981	R J Smith
1920	G A Keeley	1951	T S Bolton	1982	D E Wood
1921	J D Carpenter	1952	G H Ball	1983	R M Allan
1922	R Mook	1953	F W Veale	1984	J Mullen
1923	G Sherrington	1954	N P Vanderbilt	1985	W C Backhouse
1924	G Sherrington	1955	W McMurray	1986	B L Greenwood
1925	C H Taylor	1956	T Garstang	1987	H G Noad
1926	A F Darrah	1957	R W Barraclough	1988	G H Attwood
1927	J M T Reynolds	1958	J W Rayner MBE	1989	F A Hennessy
1928	J M T Reynolds	1959	L Rushton	1990	G P Owen
1929	L F Rowlandson	1960	H L Greenwood	1991	D M Cox
1930	M E Bishop	1961	J Moody	1992	J R Walls
1931	H S Collinge	1962	H S Collinge	1993	J J Simmons
1932	A Poirrette	1963	N H Gough	1994	G C Hinds
1933	W R H Gibbs	1964	F Beck	1995	D Hindle
1934	H Davies	1965	E B Taylor	1996	G D Anderson
1935	J A W Hepburn	1966	J B Mawdsley	1997	G C Kendrick
1936	J A W Hepburn	1967	W Sawyer	1998	G Brunskill
1937	G Worsley	1968	W B Allison DFC	1999	I W McKittrick
1938	A Crampton	1969	T Johnson	2000	R A Hennessy
1939	J Carson	1970	J B Proctor	2001	I A McDiarmid
1940	J Carson	1971	J D Giddens	2002	G A Charnock
1941	J M T Reynolds	1972	H V Bateson	2003	B G Crilly
1942	J M T Reynolds	1973	J Maher	2004	C E Pennington
1943	J M T Reynolds	1974	J A A Bent	2005	J A Proctor
1944	G Dixon	1975	T E Broughton	2006	D Lanigan
1945	G Dixon	1976	K N Owen	2007	K R Parkinson
1946	B Turner	1977	J McAlister MBE	2008	J A Taylor
1947	C Hodkinson MBE	1978	Dr C F Wilson	2009	D K Dixon
1948	C Hodkinson MBE	1979	J E Mawdsley	2010	P Molloy
1949	J Moody	1980	G C Lindsay		

The Honours Board
Lady Captains

Year	Name	Year	Name	Year	Name
1921	Mrs J Hargreave	1951	Miss G Plummer	1981	Mrs G R Tebble
1922	Mrs J Hargreave	1952	Mrs G R Creer	1982	Mrs J D Giddens
1923	Mrs J Hargreave	1953	Mrs C Prince	1983	Miss B J Brown
1924	Mrs E Ferguson	1954	Mrs H L Greenwood	1984	Mrs H Cranswick
1925	Mrs E Ferguson	1955	Mrs W Collinge	1985	Mrs D Jenkins
1926	Mrs L Bon Bernard	1956	Mrs H W Bankes	1986	Mrs J L Parkes
1927	Mrs L Bon Bernard	1957	Miss H Boardman	1987	Mrs F A Hennessy
1928	Miss E Buckley	1958	Mrs S Oddy	1988	Mrs S J Geoghegan
1929	Mrs W E Bentham	1959	Mrs N Edge	1989	Mrs K Seward
1930	Miss V C Beckett	1960	Mrs T Garstang	1990	Mrs Z H Sawyer
1931	Mrs M Hooper	1961	Mrs N P Vanderbilt	1991	Mrs E Naylor
1932	Mrs H P Whittaker	1962	Mrs B M Foster	1992	Mrs J M Davis
1933	Miss K H Kelk	1963	Mrs J E Howie	1993	Mrs S Allan
1934	Mrs J G Wheatley	1964	Mrs A Moores	1994	Mrs T W Marshall
1935	Mrs J T Marshall	1965	Mrs J Nicholl	1995	Mrs J E Cutts
1936	Miss D Aveyard	1966	Mrs C Swift	1996	Mrs J A Proctor
1937	Mrs J Leadbetter	1967	Mrs T E Hawkins	1997	Mrs S A Cobb
1938	Mrs A M Bell	1968	Mrs S G Schofield	1998	Mrs B G Crilly
1939	Mrs J Carson	1969	Mrs R N Norfolk	1999	Mrs J R Willocks
1940	Mrs J Carson	1970	Mrs A R Lucas	2000	Mrs B B Taylor
1941	Mrs H McKerrow	1971	Mrs G C Lloyd	2001	Mrs W A Turnbull
1942	Mrs A Crampton	1972	Mrs H Newsome	2002	Mrs G Hough
1943	Mrs W Lowther	1973	Mrs J O Massam	2003	Mrs H Priestley
1944	Mrs C Godwin	1974	Mrs W P Pearson	2004	Mrs J M Hewitt
1945	Mrs C L Hetherwick	1975	Mrs J A Ostenfeld	2005	Mrs T R M Newton
1946	Miss S H Southworth	1976	Mrs W Sawyer	2006	Mrs P Green
1947	Mrs G Hoyle	1977	Mrs W Dickinson	2007	Mrs B Anderson
1948	Mrs G Hoyle	1978	Mrs J E Mawdsley	2008	Mrs A G Leonard
1949	Mrs M Wilson	1979	Mrs C H Marsland	2009	Mrs J M Perkins
1950	Mrs W Marshall	1980	Mrs M J Abberley	2010	Mrs S M Foulds

Club Officers

Presidents

1919-1920	J E Hobson
1920-1921	R Mook
1921-1923	J E Hobson

Chairmen

1923-1926	G Sherrington
1926-1939	L F Rowlandson
1940-1952	A Poirette
1953-1967	H S Collinge
1967-1971	F W Veale
1971-1974	S Oddy
1974-1980	W Sawyer
1980-1983	T E Broughton
1983-1984	J McAlister MBE
1984-1985	J Mullen
1985-1986	T E Broughton
1986-1987	G H Attwood
1987-1990	G Hough
1990-1994	J D Giddens
1994-1995	G C C Lindsay
1995-1999	E W Wall
1999-2002	G Taylor
2002-2007	G Brunskill
2007-	P Halsall

Secretaries

1921	T B Wilson
1921-1924	N F R Lodge
1925-1927	Maj J S Fairclough
1927-1951	H W Davies
1952-1953	A H Dawson
1953-1958	J A W Hepburn
1958	Capt J H A Durham
1958-1962	F Hall
1962-1964	Air Com F Pearce
1964-1967	Sdn Ldr L H Clint
1967-1968	G B Sharpe
1969-1974	W R Freyer
1975-1977	G T Sumner
1978-1979	R Lucas
1980-1983	A Cunningham
1984-1992	P W Ray
1992-2006	J Graham
2006-	S H Newland

International and County Honours

English International Players

	Period	Played	Won	Halved	Lost
M P D Walls	1980-1985	25	15	0	6

England Boys

R Rook	1935	M P D Walls	1969
W S M Rooke	1968	P Kenyon	1988

England Youth

W S M Rooke   1971

England Girls

C Eckersley	1971	3	2	0	1

Lancashire County Players

	Period	Played	Won	Halved	Lost
C Blackshaw	1951-1958	7	5	0	2
G Rimmer	1965	1	0	0	1
W S M Rooke	1970-1974	17	6	1	10
M G Pearson	1975	1	0	1	0
M P D Walls	1979-1985	65	43	8	14
R I Godley	1981-1986	15	8	2	5
S G Ashcroft	1988	3	1	0	2
P Williams	1988-1991	12	5	2	5
P Kenyon	1993-2001	15	7	1	7
S J Taylor	1995	5	3	0	2
M Prue	1999	12	8	0	4
D Belch	2002-2006	23	12	2	9

Other Hillside members have played for Lancashire, but are listed by the county as members of their other clubs.

Lancashire Ladies

C Eckersley 1970

Captain's Prize

1923	R Bolton	1953	T Wilson	1983	P Hancock
1924	J E Rothwell	1954	H J Collins	1984	D J Thomson
1925	H Southorn-Laws	1955	T E Hawkins	1985	J Sciarrini
1926	T C Macaulay	1956	C F Penney	1986	D M Rose
1927	A Poirrette	1957	K Hepburn	1987	J Hepworth
1928	F Ambrose	1958	G P Roberts	1988	D M Prue
1929	H S Collinge	1959	G G Brudenell	1989	R A Hennessy
1930	R Bolton	1960	W Crowther	1990	D M Rose
1931	R Rook	1961	G P Roberts	1991	R I Godley
1932	H S Collinge	1962	W B Allison DFC	1992	J McAlister MBE
1933	E Griffith	1963	J A Ord	1993	I Lewis
1934	J P Owens	1964	T Wilson	1994	G W Ackers
1935	J Leadbeater	1965	W B Allison DFC	1995	J Sciarrini
1936	G Worsley	1966	M J Howard	1996	M R Bell
1937	J R J M Marsh	1967	J D Giddens	1997	D H Barnes
1938	W R Simister	1968	H E Swash	1998	R Leney
1939	R Swift	1969	B Hazard	1999	R C Locke
1940	E Grimes	1970	J Hockaday	2000	D G Halsall
1941	H S Collinge	1971	J C Bright	2001	R A Hennessy
1942	J P Owens	1972	G J Bromilow	2002	S Gogerty
1943	E Grimes	1973	W S M Rooke	2003	G A Charnock
1944	B Middlebrook	1974	G White	2004	A A Mather
1945	J E Wood	1975	J Handley	2005	R Berry
1946	J B Bolton	1976	R I Godley	2006	C Norbury
1947	A M Foulkes	1977	R I Godley	2007	R I Godley
1948	C Blackshaw	1978	P G Buckels	2008	R I Godley
1949	W J McMurray	1979	F A Hennessy	2009	R N Blundell
1950	T R Cummins	1980	R I Godley	2010	G A Tomlinson
1951	J R J M Marsh	1981	M L Howard		
1952	T Wilson	1982	D M Rose		

Rowlandson Trophy

1933	W D Crellin	1964	J C Brignal	1988	B Fishwick
1934	J R J M Marsh	1965	J M Bennett	1989	R D Backhouse
1935	Chas Moores	1966	J E Godley	1990	M J Harris
1936	D C Andrew	1967	W E Millard	1991	C P Hodgson
1937	B Turner	1968	A Goughlin	1992	T Martland
1938	A P Poirrette	1969	J E Godley	1993	G P Owen
1946	C A Atkinson	1970	T J Maher	1994	R K Barker
1947	F W Veale	1971	G R Keeton	1995	P Goodwin
1948	N P Vanderbilt	1972	D A Roberts	1996	J A Fitzpatrick OBE
1949	H T Hooper	1973	M J Whitaker	1997	D Lanigan
1950	F H Torpey	1974	T M Buckels	1998	K E Diamond
1951	C Blackshaw	1975	C Court	1999	R D Backhouse
1952	C F Penney	1976	G C Lindsay	2000	W Robinson
1953	R Rimmer	1977	F N Davies	2001	M L Howard
1954	C Blackshaw	1978	P Robinson	2002	H Peterson
1955	P B Bourton	1979	W Dickinson	2003	M Leary
1956	J Briggs	1980	P Hancock	2004	C A Court
1957	H W Bankes	1981	M Davis	2005	M Rothlisberger
1958	H N James	1982	D Swash	2006	R C Locke
1959	C A Fawcitt	1983	J Coyle	2007	G A Tomlinson
1960	K Hepburn	1984	R Murray	2008	K M Dalglish
1961	J B Whiteside	1985	G P Owen	2009	N A Thomson
1962	W Dickinson	1986	R K Barker	2010	D M Rose
1963	R Rimmer	1987	W F Rainford		

Founders' Trophy

1934	G Worsley	1964	G P Owen	1988	A Smith
1935	C Hodkinson	1965	J A A Bent	1989	G C Kendrick
1936	G Liptrot	1966	W Dickinson	1990	A Smith
1937	H Davies	1967	H V Bateson	1991	S D Puckey
1938	R Gardner	1968	D A Hamer	1992	G E Whittaker
1939	L Freedman	1969	A N Fell	1993	S Gogerty
1940	R Bolton	1970	C G Tattler	1994	J Leney
1941	E B Robertson	1971	H E Swash	1995	I Gardner
1948	F Bircher	1972	J A A Bent	1996	I J Newell
1949	A M Hoyle	1973	F F Dumbleton	1997	R A Maund
1950	W B Allison	1974	E H Houghton	1998	G A Charnock
1951	C Blackshaw	1975	R J Smith	1999	M L Howard
1952	W F Butterworth	1976	I Crawford	2000	M Prue
1953	W McMurray	1977	J Simmons	2001	A D Hansen
1954	H N James	1978	P G Buckels	2002	R J Howgego
1955	F Ambrose	1979	J Walsh	2003	I Lewis
1956	W Dickinson	1980	P G Buckels	2004	E Canavan
1957	R Scott	1981	G C C Lindsay	2005	D McGrath
1958	V Kettle	1982	F Hennessy	2006	P R J Cutts
1959	J M Carter	1983	P Moore	2007	M L Howard
1960	L A Wareham	1984	I Gardner	2008	J G Helsby
1961	D Redman	1985	J D Giddens	2009	D J Thomson
1962	E Wallace	1986	M L Howard	2010	S G Mather
1963	J W Leivesley	1987	T A Harrison		

Major Events

Piccadilly Medal Tournament	1962
England & Wales Ladies County Final	1968
Boys Amateur Championship	1970
English Open Amateur Stroke Play Championship (Formerly Brabazon Trophy)	1971
Piccadilly Medal Tournament	1972
Benson & Hedges Match Play Championship	1973
The PGA International Cup Match	1975
The Ladies British Open Championship	1977
The Home International Championship	1977
The Amateur Championship	1979
English Open Amateur Stroke Play Championship (Formerly Brabazon Trophy)	1981
Sun Alliance PGA Championship	1982
The English Amateur Championship	1986
International European Amateur Championship	1991
English Open Amateur Stroke Play Championship (Formerly Brabazon Trophy)	1995
The Mid-Amateur Championship	1996
The Boys Amateur Championship	2000
The English Seniors Open Championship	2003
European Mens Team Championship	2005
Home International Championship	2009

F W Veale Trophy

1986	J McGlone	1995	W Robinson	2004	J J Bradburn
1987	R A Hennessy	1996	G Brunskill	2005	C Norbury
1988	G Easton	1997	I J Newell	2006	J M Thomas
1989	D Newton	1998	R Williamson	2007	J S Rawley
1990	E Newton	1999	D J O'Connor	2008	J G Helsby
1991	J B Whiteside	2000	W R Perkins	2009	R N Blundell
1992	J McAlister MBE	2001	D M Rose	2010	K M Dalglish
1993	J Walsh	2002	A Wakefield		
1994	C P Hodgson	2003	M J Whiteside		

H S Collinge Trophy

1986	K R Parkinson	1995	B Kenyon	2004	M D Roberts
1987	A P Marsh	1996	R I Godley	2005	E Newton
1988	R I Godley	1997	D A Harkness	2006	S Kenyon
1989	S D Prue	1998	J P Moore	2007	J G Kenah
1990	J Pike	1999	M L Widders	2008	J W Helm
1991	C A Court	2000	D T Hillsdon	2009	J J Simmons
1992	J Roberts	2001	E Newton	2010	R Gillespie
1993	P G McNulty	2002	D Ainsworth		
1994	R J Smith	2003	J B Pimlott		

Hugh Davies Memorial Trophy

1954	C Blackshaw	1973	J C Cockcroft	1992	E W Wall
1955	J E Howie	1974	J M Swann	1993	J McGlone
1956	D A Rodger	1975	W R Pennington	1994	L D Hannah
1957	H V O Hughes	1976	P McCormack	1995	M Flynn
1958	J E Haworth	1977	R I Godley	1996	J P Moore
1959	T Johnson	1978	P G Buckels	1997	I J Newell
1960	J M Whiteside	1979	J Handley	1998	D J Croft
1961	T Wilson	1980	W Robinson	1999	G W Ackers
1962	F P Wilson	1981	M Evans	2000	D R Kelly
1963	E Houghton	1982	I R Turnbull	2001	P J Goodwin
1964	J Ball	1983	T Forrester	2002	J G Helsby
1965	J B Mawdsley	1984	J Handley	2003	O Pau
1966	C P Martin	1985	M S Hennessy	2004	P Williams
1967	G Hughes	1986	J E Cutts	2005	G A Tomlinson
1968	D E Goggin	1987	M D Houghton	2006	M D Roberts
1969	J Ball	1988	M R Whalen	2007	R J Mace
1970	D A Budgett	1989	F A Hennessy	2008	R N Blundell
1971	G E Leigh	1990	I J Newell	2009	F McLachlan
1972	G White	1991	J C Williamson	2010	B J Taylor

Ted Macavoy Trophy

1974	J Pike	1987	H Priestley	2000	D W Wall
1975	H James	1988	J Walsh	2001	N Dixon
1976	R M Allan	1989	W J McMurray	2002	L V Rushworth
1977	P Hancock	1990	J R Willocks	2003	J M Blundell
1978	P G Buckels	1991	A J Davies	2004	D G Holt
1979	R H Dickinson	1992	D A Budgett	2005	P R J Cutts
1980	P Craven	1993	P Kenyon	2006	S Marsden
1981	G Moss	1994	R I Godley	2007	C A Court
1982	P Paton	1995	K R Parkinson	2008	M D Roberts
1983	E Cawley	1996	M J Hannon	2009	P R Cook
1984	M J Whiteside	1997	J H Hepworth	2010	A J Marr
1985	P S Irlam	1998	D W Wall		
1986	J Leney	1999	J P Moore		

Hodkinson Scratch Trophy

1947	J R Wroe	73	1970	P Hancock	79	1989	R I Godley	152
1948	J R Wroe	71		W S M Rooke		1990	R I Godley	146
1949	C Blackshaw	72	1971	J McAlister MBE	73	1991	P Williams	149
1950	C Blackshaw	72	1972	M G Pearson	74	1992	P Williams	145
1951	C Blackshaw	74	1973	J Handley	76	1993	P Williams	149
1952	C Blackshaw	72		M G Pearson		1994	P G Buckels	152
1953	C Blackshaw	72		J S Swann		1995	P G Buckels	147
1954	C Blackshaw	75	1974	W S M Rooke	72	1996	P C Kenyon	149
1955	H N James	73	1975	J McAlister MBE	75	1997	R A Maund	150
1956	G P Roberts	71	1976	B Campbell	73	1998	P C Kenyon	149
1957	G Rimmer	76	1977	P G Buckels	75	1999	M L Howard	148
1958	T Wilson	82	1978	P G Buckels	78	2000	M E Prue	146
1959	G P Roberts	71	1979	R I Godley	77	2001	A D Hansen	151
1960	G P Roberts	71	1980	P G Buckels	146	2002	R I Godley	152
1961	G P Roberts	73	1981	G White	166	2003	R I Godley	145
1962	A K Gupta	73		C F Wilson		2004	M L Howard	151
1963	W Dickinson	75	1982	M P D Walls	148	2005	A Phillips	157
1964	H E Swash	75	1983	R I Godley	153	2006	R N Blundell	154
1965	H E Swash	75	1984	R I Godley	146	2007	R N Blundell	145
1966	G Rimmer	79	1985	P G Buckels	153	2008	R N Blundell	150
1967	G Rimmer	77	1986	M L Howard	154	2009	R Gillespie	143
1968	E D Sinclair	72	1987	P G Buckels	150	2010	R N Blundell	149
1969	A Topham	87	1988	H E Swash	154			

F W Veale Trophy

1986	J McGlone	1995	W Robinson	2004	J J Bradburn
1987	R A Hennessy	1996	G Brunskill	2005	C Norbury
1988	G Easton	1997	I J Newell	2006	J M Thomas
1989	D Newton	1998	R Williamson	2007	J S Rawley
1990	E Newton	1999	D J O'Connor	2008	J G Helsby
1991	J B Whiteside	2000	W R Perkins	2009	R N Blundell
1992	J McAlister MBE	2001	D M Rose	2010	K M Dalglish
1993	J Walsh	2002	A Wakefield		
1994	C P Hodgson	2003	M J Whiteside		

H S Collinge Trophy

1986	K R Parkinson	1995	B Kenyon	2004	M D Roberts
1987	A P Marsh	1996	R I Godley	2005	E Newton
1988	R I Godley	1997	D A Harkness	2006	S Kenyon
1989	S D Prue	1998	J P Moore	2007	J G Kenah
1990	J Pike	1999	M L Widders	2008	J W Helm
1991	C A Court	2000	D T Hillsdon	2009	J J Simmons
1992	J Roberts	2001	E Newton	2010	R Gillespie
1993	P G McNulty	2002	D Ainsworth		
1994	R J Smith	2003	J B Pimlott		

Hugh Davies Memorial Trophy

1954	C Blackshaw	1973	J C Cockcroft	1992	E W Wall
1955	J E Howie	1974	J M Swann	1993	J McGlone
1956	D A Rodger	1975	W R Pennington	1994	L D Hannah
1957	H V O Hughes	1976	P McCormack	1995	M Flynn
1958	J E Haworth	1977	R I Godley	1996	J P Moore
1959	T Johnson	1978	P G Buckels	1997	I J Newell
1960	J M Whiteside	1979	J Handley	1998	D J Croft
1961	T Wilson	1980	W Robinson	1999	G W Ackers
1962	F P Wilson	1981	M Evans	2000	D R Kelly
1963	E Houghton	1982	I R Turnbull	2001	P J Goodwin
1964	J Ball	1983	T Forrester	2002	J G Helsby
1965	J B Mawdsley	1984	J Handley	2003	O Pau
1966	C P Martin	1985	M S Hennessy	2004	P Williams
1967	G Hughes	1986	J E Cutts	2005	G A Tomlinson
1968	D E Goggin	1987	M D Houghton	2006	M D Roberts
1969	J Ball	1988	M R Whalen	2007	R J Mace
1970	D A Budgett	1989	F A Hennessy	2008	R N Blundell
1971	G E Leigh	1990	I J Newell	2009	F McLachlan
1972	G White	1991	J C Williamson	2010	B J Taylor

Lonen Cup

1933	A M Foulkes	1964	V S Carney	1988	S A Cobb
1934	R S Horne	1965	G A Swettenham	1989	A B Cunningham
1935	W Garlick	1966	S J Geoghegan	1990	S A Cobb
1936	C A Bell	1967	J E Mawdsley	1991	J P Marsh
1937	W Clough	1968	W J Hillsdon	1992	M R Helme
1938	E R Bryson	1969	R Humphrey	1993	F N Davies
1939	H W Derbyshire	1970	H W Briscoe	1994	J Simms
1946	J Reynolds	1971	N Hindson	1995	B Shipton
1947	W B Allison	1972	H Ryland	1996	J A Fitzpatrick OBE
1948	S G White	1973	G Moss	1997	J Bolton
1949	G G Brudenell	1974	A Davies	1998	J A Proctor
1950	J T McCabe	1975	J Forshaw	1999	G Whiteside
1951	W E P Wilson	1976	E W Wall	2000	J G Barrack
1952	J Carr	1977	G R Brown	2001	P Moore
1953	S L Dean		F Irvine	2002	T L Griffiths
1954	A E Reece	1978	C J Schofield	2003	M R Helme
1955	S D Cross	1979	P S Irlam	2004	G Whiteside
1956	J T McCabe	1980	S Taylor	2005	G S Jones
1957	A Barrett	1981	N Jackson	2006	R Berry
1958	J Naylor	1982	W J Parkinson	2007	J W Helm
1959	W J Hillsdon	1983	S A Cobb	2008	J Roberts
1960	C D Martin	1984	D Mayman	2009	J G Barrack
1961	G A Long	1985	J Armstrong	2010	J W Helm
1962	W R Wilkinson	1986	W R Pennington		
1963	J Jackman	1987	I Maguire		

Mike Buckels Match Play Trophy

1967	W Dickinson	1982	M Howard	1997	D Kelly
1968	T M Buckels	1983	R Cromack	1998	D Wright
1969	G Rimmer	1984	H E Swash	1999	P Molloy
1970	N Dodson	1985	M P D Walls	2000	D G Halsall
1971	G Rimmer	1986	A McPhee	2001	R A Maund
1972	P Bint	1987	B G Dyson	2002	G Taylor
1973	P Bint	1988	R I Godley	2003	D M Prue
1974	P Bint	1989	R A Hennessy	2004	G L Carr
1975	J C Bright	1990	G Rimmer	2005	D Hillsdon
1976	M D Houghton	1991	B Kenyon	2006	R J Mace
1977	P Hancock	1992	E Cawley	2007	A Pike
1978	R I Godley	1993	P Kenyon	2008	C E Pennington
1979	M P D Walls	1994	R A Maund	2009	J P Moore
1980	M P D Walls	1995	P Walker	2010	P Janssen
1981	P Hancock	1996	R A Hennessy		

Malies Cup

Year	Name	Year	Name	Year	Name
1926	E Crosby	1959	M Albert	1986	K J Winrow
1927	G A Keeley	1960	A K Mercer	1987	M Pickles
1928	W A Dyson	1961	W P Pearson	1988	A G Leonard
1929	W Wright	1962	K Hepburn	1989	S J Goodwin
1930	H S Collinge	1963	H E Swash	1990	G P Owen
1931	A Poirrette	1964	W N Jones	1991	J Armstrong
1932	E Poirrette	1965	F W Veale	1992	J R Mulvey
1933	I E Mottram	1966	J P Diesen	1993	K J Winrow
1934	F N Whitaker	1967	J Handley	1994	B G Crilly
1935	M E Bishop	1968	T M Buckels	1995	D Barnes
1936	C A Ball	1969	J P Quinn	1996	K J Winrow
1937	J A Lewis	1970	K A Lawson	1997	D M Prue
1938	A N Tasker	1971	G E Leigh	1998	R Cator
1939	C A Johnson	1972	D A Roberts	1999	D R S Bald
1946	J R Wroe	1973	G Easton	2000	G H Strong
1947	F W Veale	1974	J Bolton	2001	E W Ellis
1948	F F Oldfield	1975	J Coyle	2002	K R Parkinson
1949	A L R Cross	1976	W J Parkinson	2003	R D Clifford
1950	L W Barras	1977	T M Buckels	2004	J J Bradburn
1951	N P Vanderbilt	1978	D F Dean	2005	J P Moore
1952	H R Mason	1979	C Melling	2006	D W Wright
1953	J E Haworth	1980	D Roberts	2007	P Edgeller
1954	J M Howie	1981	H W Briscoe	2008	J G Helsby
1955	J Carey	1982	J McMurray	2009	A D Hansen
1956	K M MacIntosh	1983	J E Mawdsley	2010	L V Rushworth
1957	T E Hawkins	1984	E Cawley		
1958	H R Blevin	1985	M S Hennessy		

Aggregate Trophy

1931	A Batty	1958	W Dickinson	1986	I R Turnbull
1932	A N Tasker	1959	A K Gupta	1987	R I Godley
1933	H S Collinge	1960	F Hall	1988	G Rimmer
1934	G Worsley	1961	R Rimmer	1989	T J Devaney
1935	W T Ellis	1962	A K Gupta	1990	G Taylor
1936	D Taylor	1963	R Rimmer	1991	D M Prue
1937	R Gardner	1964	G Rimmer	1992	P G Buckels
	A N Tasker	1965	J Ball	1993	I R Callaghan MBE
1938	W Marshall	1966	G Rimmer	1994	R A Maund
1939	C Blackshaw	1967	W S M Rooke	1995	J Sciarrini
1940	J T Lucas	1968	K N Owen	1996	D B Turner
1941	J A Lewis	1969	H E Swash	1997	I J Newell
1942	J A Lewis	1970	C F Wilson	1998	M L Howard
1943	F Hall	1971	M G Pearson	1999	A Pike
1944	J E Wood	1972	F N Davies	2000	R A Hennessy
1945	A Harrison	1973	F F Dumbleton	2001	A J Davies
1946	H V O Hughes	1974	P Hancock	2002	P Williams
1947	H J Collins	1975	G Rimmer	2003	D G Halsall
1948	T E Hawkins	1976	R A Maund	2004	C Norbury
1949	J R Wroe	1977	J J Simmons	2005	A J Davies
1950	W E R Gunthorpe	1978	J C Cockcroft	2006	R Gillespie
1951	A M Hoyle	1979	R I Godley	2007	R J Mace
1952	A E Charnley	1980	R I Godley	2008	J G Helsby
1953	R Rimmer	1981	J J Simmons	2009	R J Mace
1954	C Blackshaw	1982	P Forshaw	2010	W R Perkins
1955	B Shaw	1983	T L Griffiths		G A Tomlinson
1956	W Dickinson	1984	W Robinson		
1957	B Shaw	1985	A J Davies		

Ladies - Best Scratch Score

1931	Miss N Hunt	84	1960	Mrs H W Bankes	83	1985	Miss P Smillie	73
1932	Miss N Hunt	82		Mrs T E Hawkins		1986	Miss P Smillie	75
1933	Miss M Berry	85	1961	Mrs T E Hawkins	83	1987	Mrs B Kenyon	82
	Miss I Schofield			Mrs A Moores		1988	Mrs B Kenyon	83
1934	Miss N Hunt	83	1962	Mrs A Moores	78	1989	Mrs B Kenyon	81
1935	Miss N Hunt	81	1963	Mrs H W Bankes	83	1990	Mrs B Kenyon	81
1936	Miss N Hunt	81	1964	Mrs A Moores	84	1991	Mrs B Kenyon	81
1937	Mrs A M Bell	84	1965	Mrs T E Hawkins	83		Mrs H Priestley	
1938	Miss V J Beckett	84	1966	Mrs J Nicholl	87	1992	Mrs B Kenyon	79
	Mrs J C Bebbington		1967	Mrs H W Bankes	83	1993	Mrs B Kenyon	79
1945	Miss K H Kelk	84	1968	Mrs A Moores	85	1994	Mrs B Kenyon	77
1946	Mrs J C Bebbington	82	1969	Miss C Eckersley	85	1995	Mrs B Kenyon	76
1947	Mrs H W Bankes	80	1970	Miss C Eckersley	77	1996	Mrs B Kenyon	75
1948	Mrs H W Bankes	81	1971	Miss C Eckersley	79	1997	Mrs B Kenyon	76
1949	Mrs H W Bankes	80	1972	Miss C Eckersley	76	1998	Mrs B Kenyon	82
1950	Mrs H W Bankes	80	1973	Mrs H W Curtis	81	1999	Mrs B Kenyon	78
1951	Mrs H W Bankes	82	1974	Mrs H W Curtis	85	2000	Mrs B Kenyon	78
1952	Mrs H W Bankes	78	1975	Mrs W Sawyer	86	2001	Mrs B Kenyon	82
	Mrs G Hoyle		1976	Mrs F Halstead	84		Mrs J M Davis	
1953	Mrs H W Bankes	74		Mrs H W Curtis		2002	Mrs B Kenyon	79
1954	Mrs G Hoyle	79	1977	Mrs W Sawyer	81	2003	Mrs B Kenyon	75
1955	Mrs H W Bankes	80		Mrs E Thomson		2004	Miss H Nolan	77
1956	Mrs H W Bankes	78	1978	Mrs H W Curtis	86	2005	Mrs B Kenyon	81
1957	Mrs H W Bankes	81	1979	Mrs W Sawyer	86	2006	Mrs B Kenyon	82
	Mrs T E Hawkins		1980	Mrs H W Curtis	86	2007	Mrs B Kenyon	80
1958	Mrs H W Bankes	84	1981	Miss P Smillie	76		Miss A Thornberry	
	Mrs A Moores		1982	Miss P Smillie	82	2008	Mrs A Sanderson	82
1959	Mrs H W Bankes	81	1983	Miss P Smillie	78	2009	Miss H Nolan	80
	Mrs A Moores		1984	Mrs Z H Sawyer	84	2010	Mrs R C Wood	85

Ladies - Lil Lucas Trophy

1972	Mrs W Sawyer	1985	Mrs B Carter	1998	Mrs J E Cutts
1973	Mrs E E Garstang	1986	Mrs H Cranswick	1999	Mrs V Heald Jones
1974	Mrs A E Roberts	1987	Mrs J G Hewitt	2000	Mrs H N James
1975	Mrs G Rimmer	1988	Mrs J E Cutts	2001	Mrs J K Maund
1976	Mrs F Halstead	1989	Mrs B Kenyon	2002	Mrs A Turner
1977	Mrs W Sawyer	1990	Mrs M A Carter	2003	Mrs P Bennett
1978	Mrs M J Howard	1991	Mrs J D Giddens	2004	Mrs A Turner
1979	Mrs J G Hewitt	1992	Mrs J D Giddens	2005	Mrs S Rimmer
1980	Mrs H W Curtis	1993	Mrs P Green	2006	Mrs A Ellis
1981	Mrs M J Howard	1994	Mrs J Hewitt	2007	Miss A Thornberry
1982	Mrs A C Roberts	1995	Mrs J Jaeger	2008	Mrs A Sanderson
1983	Mrs G Moss	1996	Mrs G Pearson	2009	Mrs S E M Williams
1984	Mrs H N James	1997	Mrs J C Cawley	2010	Mrs P Green

Aggregate Trophy

1931	A Batty	1958	W Dickinson	1986	I R Turnbull
1932	A N Tasker	1959	A K Gupta	1987	R I Godley
1933	H S Collinge	1960	F Hall	1988	G Rimmer
1934	G Worsley	1961	R Rimmer	1989	T J Devaney
1935	W T Ellis	1962	A K Gupta	1990	G Taylor
1936	D Taylor	1963	R Rimmer	1991	D M Prue
1937	R Gardner	1964	G Rimmer	1992	P G Buckels
	A N Tasker	1965	J Ball	1993	I R Callaghan MBE
1938	W Marshall	1966	G Rimmer	1994	R A Maund
1939	C Blackshaw	1967	W S M Rooke	1995	J Sciarrini
1940	J T Lucas	1968	K N Owen	1996	D B Turner
1941	J A Lewis	1969	H E Swash	1997	I J Newell
1942	J A Lewis	1970	C F Wilson	1998	M L Howard
1943	F Hall	1971	M G Pearson	1999	A Pike
1944	J E Wood	1972	F N Davies	2000	R A Hennessy
1945	A Harrison	1973	F F Dumbleton	2001	A J Davies
1946	H V O Hughes	1974	P Hancock	2002	P Williams
1947	H J Collins	1975	G Rimmer	2003	D G Halsall
1948	T E Hawkins	1976	R A Maund	2004	C Norbury
1949	J R Wroe	1977	J J Simmons	2005	A J Davies
1950	W E R Gunthorpe	1978	J C Cockcroft	2006	R Gillespie
1951	A M Hoyle	1979	R I Godley	2007	R J Mace
1952	A E Charnley	1980	R I Godley	2008	J G Helsby
1953	R Rimmer	1981	J J Simmons	2009	R J Mace
1954	C Blackshaw	1982	P Forshaw	2010	W R Perkins
1955	B Shaw	1983	T L Griffiths		G A Tomlinson
1956	W Dickinson	1984	W Robinson		
1957	B Shaw	1985	A J Davies		

Lady Captain's Prize

1922	Miss E Lawrenson	1954	Mrs T Garstang	1984	Mrs E Thomson
1923	Mrs E Ferguson	1955	Mrs C Blackshaw	1985	Mrs W P Pearson
1925	Miss G Plummer	1956	Mrs H Newsome	1986	Miss P Smillie
1926	Miss M Threlfall	1957	Mrs W Dickinson	1987	Mrs P J McCormack
1927	Mrs W E Bentham	1958	Mrs J F Cunningham	1988	Mrs E Thomson
1928	Miss N Walker	1959	Mrs J S Simpson	1989	Mrs G Moss
1929	Miss M Berry	1960	Mrs B M Foster	1990	Mrs B Kenyon
1930	Miss E Buckley	1961	Mrs T E Hawkins	1991	Mrs S A Cobb
1931	Miss N Hunt	1962	Mrs T Garstang	1992	Ms S Smith Crallan
1932	Mrs R Rook	1963	Mrs T E Hawkins	1993	Miss P Butler
1933	Mrs E Griffith	1964	Mrs H W Bankes	1994	Mrs P Green
1934	Miss N Walker	1965	Mrs J C Hanley	1995	Mrs B Carter
1935	Miss D Aveyard	1966	Mrs A R Lucas	1996	Mrs K J Winrow
1936	Miss V C Beckett	1967	Mrs T Garstang	1997	Mrs P H Prince
1937	Miss D Aveyard	1968	Mrs F K Morrall	1998	Mrs J Hansen
1938	Miss K H Kelk	1969	Mrs C H Marsland	1999	Mrs P Green
1940	Miss E Lee	1970	Mrs C H Marsland	2000	Mrs J Jaeger
1941	Mrs B C Stanley	1971	Mrs G M Hartley	2001	Mrs J M Davis
1942	Mrs H McKerrow	1972	Mrs A Coughlin	2002	Mrs A Turner
1943	Mrs J Greenwood	1973	Mrs K Seward	2003	Mrs S Prue
1944	Mrs B C Stanley	1974	Mrs W Sawyer	2004	Mrs S L Armstrong
1945	Mrs J C Bebbington	1975	Mrs M J Howard	2005	Mrs M Parkes
1946	Mrs J C Bebbington	1976	Mrs J Hewitt	2006	Mrs J Priestley
1947	Mrs H W Bankes	1977	Mrs J D Giddens	2007	Mrs J H Whitehead
1948	Miss Pam Rook	1978	Mrs O Butterworth	2008	Mrs K A Helme
1949	Miss Pam Rook	1979	Mrs J M Davis	2009	Mrs M Kenah
1950	Miss I Banks	1980	Mrs M Jenkins	2010	Mrs R C Wood
1951	Miss I Banks	1981	Mrs W Dickinson		
1952	Mrs H W Bankes	1982	Mrs H N James		
1953	Mrs J R J M Marsh	1983	Miss L McCluskey		

Ladies - Veterans Prize

1964	Mrs W N Jones	1980	Mrs A C Roberts	1996	Mrs B Kenyon
1965	Mrs T E Hawkins	1981	Mrs W P Pearson	1997	Mrs J C Cawley
1966	Mrs F G Pendergast	1982	Mrs W Dickinson	1998	Mrs S Armstrong
1967	Mrs T E Hawkins	1983	Mrs M Morrall	1999	Mrs J M Davis
1968	Mrs E S Anderton	1984	Mrs G R Allison	2000	Mrs V Heald-Jones
1969	Mrs J E Howie	1985	Mrs E Thomson	2001	Mrs W A Turnbull
1970	Mrs W Sawyer	1986	Mrs J Patten	2002	Mrs J E Cutts
1971	Mrs W R Freyer	1987	Mrs J D Giddens	2003	Mrs J E Cutts
1972	Mrs F K Morrall	1988	Mrs J D Giddens	2004	Mrs M Greenwood
1973	Mrs D Mayman	1989	Mrs F A Hennessy	2005	Mrs V Heald-Jones
1974	Mrs N Hindson	1990	Mrs J L Parkes	2006	Mrs S Rimmer
1975	Mrs L Davey	1991	Mrs M J Abberley	2007	Mrs A Ellis
1976	Mrs N Edge	1992	Mrs J D Giddens	2008	Mrs J E Cutts
1977	Mrs H Newsome	1993	Mrs J D Giddens	2009	Mrs B Scott-Wignall
1978	Mrs A C Roberts	1994	Mrs M Mallinson	2010	Mrs S M Foulds
1979	Mrs J A Ostenfeld	1995	Mrs S Rimmer		

Ladies - Smith Cup

1926	Miss N Walker	1955	Mrs A U Dalley	1984	Mrs P Mallinson
1927	Miss S A Bell	1956	Mrs C Blackshaw	1985	Mrs J Patten
1928	Mrs R Fairhurst	1957	Mrs J Nicholl	1986	Mrs J Priestley
1929	Miss V C Beckett	1958	Mrs S Oddy	1987	Mrs B Kenyon
1930	Miss B Day	1959	Mrs H Newsome	1988	Mrs K Edwards
1931	Miss E A Lawrenson	1960	Mrs J E Cunningham	1989	Mrs K Bestwick
1932	Miss M Berry	1961	Mrs B C Stanley	1990	Mrs E W Ellis
1933	Miss M Berry	1962	Mrs N H Gough	1991	Mrs H Priestley
1934	Mrs H J Flewitt	1963	Miss I Banks	1992	Mrs H Priestley
1935	Miss E Burnley Jones	1964	Mrs J O Massam	1993	Mrs B Kenyon
1936	Miss D Aveyard	1965	Mrs D Redman	1994	Mrs S Rimmer
1937	Mrs J A Godwin	1966	Mrs F T Grayer	1995	Mrs B Kenyon
1938	Mrs J Goulder	1967	Mrs H W Bankes	1996	Mrs G Pearson
1939	Mrs J C Bebbington	1968	Mrs L M Thomson	1997	Mrs G Pearson
1940	Mrs J Greenwood	1969	Mrs L M Thomson	1998	Mrs S Rimmer
1941	Mrs B C Stanley	1970	Mrs H Newsome	1999	Mrs J E Cutts
1942	Mrs C A Glass	1971	Mrs M J Howard	2000	Mrs V Heald-Jones
1943	Miss G Lee	1972	Mrs J Ostenfeld	2001	Mrs J E S Rose
1944	Mrs A N Tasker	1973	Miss E L K Gunthorpe	2002	Mrs J Croft
1945	Mrs W E Whiteley	1974	Mrs S Oddy	2003	Mrs K Nolan
1946	Mrs A Harrison	1975	Mrs W Dickinson	2004	Mrs J M Hewitt
1947	Mrs H Newsome	1976	Mrs M J Abberley	2005	Mrs J Jaeger
1948	Mrs G Hoyle	1977	Mrs E Thomson	2006	Mrs J Staines
1949	Miss Pam Rook	1978	Mrs W Dickinson	2007	Mrs T R M Newton
1950	Mrs W Greenwood	1979	Mrs W Sawyer	2008	Mrs A Sanderson
1951	Miss J C Ambrose	1980	Mrs E Thomson	2009	Mrs J H Whitehead
1952	Mrs G McKerrow	1981	Mrs J G Hewitt	2010	Ms J J Donnelly
1953	Miss G Lee	1982	Mrs G R Tebble		
1954	Mrs A Moores	1983	Mrs M Morrall		

HILLSIDE GOLF COURSE

1932

HILLSIDE GOLF COURSE

c.1940